PREPUBLICATION REVIEWS OF

PAY ATTENTION TO THE CHILDREN:

Janet Gonzalez-Mena, Author of Dragon Mom *and other child development books, Napa Valley College, Napa, CA*:
Sydney really knows her subject. Her enthusiasm bubbles right out of the book. I learned a lot.

Dr. Jeannette Veatch, Author of Key Words to Reading *and professor emerita at Arizona State University:*
Here is a book that furthers learner-centered education far beyond any current educational practice. I believe readers can use this book to support and develop their own methodology and practice. I read the galleys straight through, only pausing to sleep. This readable book deserves the widest circulation possible....It is time for a resurgence of interest in Sylvia Ashton-Warner, arguably the most gifted teacher of the twentieth century. Clemens does a superb, insightful job in researching and explaining this woman, giving us a marvelously complete and complex understanding of her.

Dr. Asa G. Hilliard, III, Fuller E. Callaway Professor of Urban Education, Georgia State University:
Reading *Pay Attention to the Children: Lessons for Teachers and Parents from Sylvia Ashton-Warner,* gave me much more understanding of this magnificent woman. I believe that this book deserves to be widely read by professionals. I am deeply concerned that the practice of teaching has become a technological exercise. While the technology is important, the human context is even more so and I believe this book helps to make that point.

PAY ATTENTION TO THE CHILDREN

Jack Shallcrass, New Zealand Educator, Friend of Sylvia Ashton-Warner:

Like Paulo Freire, Sylvia Ashton-Warner unlocked the power of the words that resonated the chords of people's personal experience. For Freire this had profound political and social implications because it was an act of liberation and a call to action to right injustices. To be able to name something was to have the power to confront it. Anything less than such liberation was oppression—there was no middle ground. For Sylvia the liberation was to free creative energy which lessened the ever-present danger of the mind erupting destructively. For Freire the logic of action was political, for Sylvia it was to preserve the knife-edge balance between individual growth and destruction. Though both believed and behaved with passionate commitment, Freire was guided by intellect and Sylvia by her heart. Freire is read and discussed predominantly in intellectual circles while one of Sylvia's gifts was to make herself and her work accessible to a wider public.

On these pages Sylvia appears as I knew her: exasperating, charming and always, like good art, with the capacity to surprise. What counts in the long run is that she touched, challenged, and surprised so many people. She made herself available at a time when such resonances were badly needed.

Sydney Gurewitz Clemens has captured all this and much more.

PAY ATTENTION TO THE CHILDREN

James T. Greenman, Early Childhood Environments Developer, Minneapolis, MN:
I really liked the quality of the writing and the content. As an educator, I know the book will be a useful addition to my library to draw upon in future. Its audience should go beyond fans of Sylvia Ashton-Warner or Sydney Gurewitz Clemens, feminists, and proponents of open education, to still more people who read the book and go forward to learn more from Sylvia Ashton-Warner and other progressive thinkers.

Dr. George Parekowhai, Professor of Maori Studies, Auckland College of Education (New Zealand/Aotearoa):
As a young Maori teacher I recognized the brilliance of Sylvia Ashton-Warner, an inspired Pakeha [white] country teacher, eliciting optimum creative responses from infant Maori learners, struggling to make sense of a confused, foreign institution called a rural Native/Maori school. Sylvia's contribution for me is the response of a sensitive teacher, entering and transforming the natural world of a Maori child, who was in search of a worthy place in the violent, hostile and competitive society of postwar, mainstream New Zealand. I found *Pay Attention to the Children: Lessons for Teachers and Parents from Sylvia Ashton-Warner,* to be a detailed, sobering, scholarly expose of her complex and often contradictory character.

Dr. Elizabeth Jones, Author of Emergent Curriculum, Teaching Adults, *and* The Play's the Thing, *Faculty, Pacific Oaks College, Pasadena, CA:*
From time to time there is a teacher who inspires a great many other teachers. Sydney Clemens's passionate regard for Sylvia Ashton-Warner as a teacher worth learning from is vividly communicated in this book.

PAY ATTENTION TO THE CHILDREN

Herbert Kohl, Author of Reading, How to *and other books about the possibilities of teaching, Point Arena, CA:*
Sydney Gurewitz Clemens' book forcibly reminds us that the work and life of Sylvia Ashton-Warner are every bit as relevant today as they were when she was writing and teaching. The book provides us with a personal and cultural portrait of Ashton-Warner that adds depth to our understanding of her as an educator. It is about literacy that comes from the heart and honors children in a way that is all too rare.

Diedra Epps-Miller, Specialist in Parent and Staff Empowerment and Urban Education, San Francisco, CA:
Sydney Gurewitz Clemens has crafted a triple treat. She has capably woven a biographical study of the enigmatic and passionate Sylvia Ashton-Warner with a readable, scholarly examination of Ashton-Warner's approach to teaching and other writings and has added her own highly illustrative observations, reflections and applications of this theory in her urban classrooms. Sydney's insight and analysis of Ashton-Warner's work and its applicability where cross-cultural teaching takes place provides the reader with a new Key Vocabulary of critical elements for authentic practice.

Clemens and Ashton-Warner effectively model the roles of teacher as researcher, as scribe and as guide, while clearly articulating a viable framework for rewarding teaching experiences. Pay attention—a simple yet profound *credo*—challenges adults to question the limits that society places on children's potential. This book is a masterful story of inquiry, discovery, exploration and validation, and I highly recommend it for Women's Studies, Teaching Reading, and Urban Education courses.

Other books by Sydney Gurewitz Clemens

THE SUN'S NOT BROKEN, A CLOUD'S JUST IN THE WAY:
ON CHILD-CENTERED TEACHING 1984

CENTERING ON THE CHILDREN 1985

Pay Attention to the Children: Lessons for Teachers and Parents from Sylvia Ashton-Warner

Sydney Gurewitz Clemens

RATTLE OK PUBLICATIONS
NAPA, CALIFORNIA

Published by
Rattle OK Publications
P.O. Box 5614
Napa, CA 94581-0614
E-mail SBE51@AOL.com
To order multiple copies call 800 253-8085
To order single copies call 415 586-7338

Printed in the United States of America

Chapter Four was printed in a slightly different form in the Claremont Reading Conference Fifth Annual Yearbook, 1990.

First Edition
0 9 8 7 6 5 4 3 2 1

Libraries of Congress Cataloging in Publication Data
Clemens, Sydney Gurewitz
Pay Attention to the Children: Lessons for Teachers and Parents from Sylvia Ashton-Warner / by Sydney Gurewitz Clemens

1. Sylvia Ashton-Warner
2. Early childhood education
3. Educational history
4. Curriculum development
5. Cross-cultural education
6. Teaching beginning reading
7. Roles of stories in human development

Library of Congress Catalog Card No. 96-70255

ISBN 1-883965-41-1

Cover illustration by Rick Lopes
Typesetting and layout by Sydney Gurewitz Clemens

CONTENTS

INTRODUCTION

The insights and teaching methods developed by Sylvia Ashton-Warner are just as relevant today as when they first came to our attention more than a generation ago. As I read this fresh and lively exposition of her experiences and the way she transformed them into an approach to working with young children, I recalled how deeply they impressed and inspired me on first reading her work in the 1960s.

Ashton-Warner's ideas are captured most succinctly by Clemens' question, "How could any insight be more pertinent to our sometimes faltering, sometimes frustrating attempts to teach ourselves how to reach, teach and learn from our increasingly diverse groups of children?"

Sylvia Ashton-Warner, by her own richly recorded accounts and the reports of those who knew her, was a complex and multidimensional woman. The contexts and conditions in which she grew as a person and as a teacher are distant from us in both time and place. It is therefore not surprising that the controversies that swirl around her as a person and as a pedagogue often detract from what can be learned from her work. Nevertheless, I am convinced that each reader can glean from Clemens' welcome exposition of her work some fundamental insights about the nature of teaching and reaching young children.

More than most, Sylvia Ashton-Warner seemed to heed Rousseau's injunction to transform our sensations into ideas. Though some of her sensations were unique to her, and perhaps difficult for many of us to appreciate, she seems to have made great use of them in generating her approach to teaching young children.

Clemens' lively account of Ashton-Warner's thought and work greatly enriches us as teachers and as participants in the development of the field of early childhood education. This book could hardly be more timely as we struggle to meet the challenge of working with increasingly diverse groups of children.

—Lilian G. Katz, Ph.D.,
Professor of Early Childhood Education
Director, ERIC/ECE
University of Illinois, Urbana-Champaign

PREFACE

Sylvia Ashton-Warner's approach to teaching has never been more needed than today in this country at a time when cultural differences severely upset urban school systems.

This book is a labor of love undertaken by a teacher sharing the wisdom she learned reading the work of her teacher. Teaching is an undervalued art demanding a fine mix of analysis and intuition. Careful observation evokes the most successful form for successful teaching. Clemens observed Ashton-Warner by reading her closely and learned from her how to evoke the response of children. This is central to developing the tools we need for survival in a multicultural, complex and therefore fascinating world.

The Vancouver Study, 1972-4, was an investigation of Ashton-Warner's methods, supervised by Dr. Selma Wasserman and Ashton-Warner herself, both on the faculty of Simon Fraser University. The study found that children learned to read as well from teachers using Key Vocabulary as from those who used traditional methods. The significant difference between the two groups was the more favorable attitude the Key Vocabulary group children had toward reading.

Children in the study "had experiences in making decisions daily, and the nature of the decision-making increased in complexity and sophistication as the program developed." And, "the expectation of the 'Organic Day' program is that children will work together cooperatively and that children will help each other when help is needed. The 'Organic Day' provides continuous opportunities for children to learn with and from each other."

In the study children used play and creative expression to work out personal and emotional issues. The study finds "the Key Vocabulary approach may also be a means by which the young child is provided with an opportunity to express in appropriate ways, his rage, his fear, his anxiety, his feelings of rejection and other pressureful concerns from his life outside the school."

All of these things Clemens learned from Ashton-Warner, and this kind of discovery enriches and moves us forward.

—Joan M. Erikson, Artist
Author, alone and in collaboration with her husband Erik, of several books on human development.

THANKS

As a writer I ask a great deal from my friends. Each of the following people read the manuscript in one or more of its many stages and helped me to tell this story:

Ingrid Andrews
Lisa Bourgeault
Carl Cheney
Bill Cole Cliett
Marna Cohen
Renatta Cooper
Susie Corbett
Sharon Elwell
Edith Levitov Garduk
Ariela Gidron
Jim Greenman

Lurilla Harris
Bev Hartman
Michael Kelly
Donna Levis
Elizabeth Maury
Patrick McClung
Alison McCormick
Joan Metge
Judy Nygren
Suzanne Pollard
Graham F. Prindle

Lore Rasmussen
Sally Roberts
Shoshanna Schwimmer
Sonya Shoptaugh
Andy Smallwood
Doris Smith
Mary Ann Sommerville
Anna Tartaglini
Laurie Todd
Terre Virgason
Susan Willard

Another group of friends helped me so much that their ideas and language have become part of my thinking and my writing:

Jeanne Marie Bear
Isobel Milton Cerney
Elizabeth Jones
Nan Narboe
Kathy Oberg

And Charles Garrigues, who stands alone in his help to me on this project. He thought my stories about Sylvia and teaching worth putting in order. Struggling with his final, awful illness, generous with his time and wisdom, Chuck, always a seeker for truth, helped me tell my stories. Any remaining disorder is because I was obstinate.

This book is dedicated to Isobel Milton Cerney, mentor and guide, the eldest member of my community, who died as I wrote this book, and to Stella Karuna, Amelia Bear and Daryl Carl Dancy, Jr., born with the book, the youngest.

ONE—DISCOVERING SYLVIA

Sheer chance to have a turn at all, to be alive. To give the journey a point you could aim to give back to life what life had given you: pick up any gems in the grass by the wayside, polish them up and hand them back when your turn is over.[1]

In 1961, when I first read Sylvia's novel, *Spinster*, I was a beginning teacher at Public School 123 in New York City, painfully dissatisfied with my work. *Spinster* shocked me into a profound change of direction. It showed me another struggling teacher trying to help children learn and grow. Like me, she wanted to preserve children's creative and diverse energies without getting herself fired. This author understood my frustration and loneliness as I struggled to learn my craft.

Sylvia Ashton-Warner is one of the mothers of early childhood education. Her work has been important to many of the thinkers who shape our current ideas of developmentally appropriate curriculum and of early literacy. She is best known for her nonfiction book, *Teacher*, which tells about her development of Key Vocabulary, a developmentally appropriate method of introducing young children to reading. Key Vocabulary instruction gives each child just those words which name that child's most vivid images, words like *mommy* and *kiss* and *ghost* and *whipping*. Chapter Four is about this work. But Sylvia Ashton-Warner's life and work teach us many other useful lessons as well.

Because Sylvia was deeply troubled (Chapter Two tells about this) she paid substantial attention to healing herself. She then discovered that what worked to heal her own life was interesting and useful to the children she taught.

She had encountered children's resistance to the prescribed curriculum and came to believe that canned, colonial curriculum did intellectual and psychic harm. As she paid attention to the particular children she taught and tried modifying curriculum to suit them, she found that she could develop good curriculum—arts curriculum—by studying children closely. (Chapter Three discusses this.)

Sylvia was a native of New Zealand, born of parents of English descent. She taught Maori children, Polynesians. The curriculum she was supposed to teach was culturally European, and ignored Maori culture. She came to see that culture is part of an individual's dignity and that to disregard a child's culture is to be disrespectful to that child and lose the opportunity to teach him or her effectively.

Sylvia was able to hold onto her sanity by taking great blocks of time to paint, sculpt, draw, play music and write. Her own experience taught her that the arts are the best way for children and adults to find balance and harmony. Chapter Five is a feminist look at her system of work.

Sylvia would not have been able to devote time to her creative work had she followed the very Victorian gender role New Zealand society prescribed. She learned to leave her own children in the care of their father and do creative work. Her husband did for her what countless wives do for their husbands as a matter of course. She asserted her right to full expression despite social pressures, sharing child-rearing with her partner, abandoning the assumption that women must put their own needs after those of all other family members.

Beginning her teaching career as a floundering disciplinarian she came to redefine the whole idea of discipline. She learned, at least in theory, that one kind of discipline comes from a benevolent, emergent curriculum and environment; that another kind of discipline comes from working with media which impose their own natural limits upon the artist; and that yet another discipline comes from keeping one's eye upon the desired achievement and making oneself take the time and energy to consistently approach that achievement. Chapters Eight and Nine examine what Sylvia did about discipline.

Somehow, along the way, she learned that the teacher can take responsibility for the problem if the learner doesn't learn the material, saying: "I didn't show you well enough." This permits more tries and, if necessary, more failures, without a total loss of confidence on the child's part.

There were many lessons for me, back in 1961, reading *Spinster.* The children Sylvia portrayed asserted themselves, cavorted and made mischief throughout her book. She was being formed by the Maori children and their parents in her community as I was being formed by the African-American children and parents in mine.

Her children, like mine, were lovely and wild, and she wasn't oppressing them but doing something else, and I was intrigued by that something else. In her books I found a commitment to dialogue and negotiation between oneself and the other, between nations, between races. The "simple" expedient of expressing our angers and fears in arts, she taught, would make us less willing to oppress or kill at the behest of our leaders. Sylvia's creative necessity led her to accept differences. Because she herself needed space to differ with received opinion she allowed such space to others. She had skills I needed. I took Sylvia Ashton-Warner with me to kindergarten and began to be a better teacher.

Learning about the historical Sylvia—by her own account a woman wounded, fighting both neurosis and custom in ways that often seemed ungainly, at times unkind—worked against my inclination to hero-worship, and left me finally with the Sylvia I needed intact. I could admire this awkward and difficult woman not just because she made a productive, dramatic life for herself against high odds, but because she saw that the odds against children in classrooms were needlessly high, and did something about it.

I continue to take inspiration from Sylvia Ashton-Warner, and I've written this book in order to clarify her influence and to explore and continue her work. I still think like a classroom teacher, which I was for some twenty years. You will hear my voice throughout this narrative speaking directly to you of my experience with children and teachers and of the many ways Sylvia influences my life.

I hope you won't read this book instead of Ashton-Warner's own books. She was a great storyteller. My book is meant to introduce the ideas Sylvia reiterated and present them in a way that makes her lessons more readily accessible. The reader who is interested in reading Sylvia's own books is invited to read Appendix III page 166, which suggests an order for reading the books.

Studying her life and work gave me insight into what it took for a woman who was a diarist, a novelist and a wife and mother, to empower herself a full generation before the women's movement of the seventies. Studying her work and life gives us clues about how she came, from unlikely beginnings, to be visible across an ocean and still timely after fifty years.

When I read *Teacher* a year or two after *Spinster*, I couldn't distinguish the fictional Anna Vorontosov, heroine of *Spinster*, from the factual Mrs. (Sylvia) Henderson, in *Teacher*, and became unsure which one needed the morning brandy. The two books overlapped—a third of the material was repeated, almost word for word. To this day, eight or ten readings later, I still have a little trouble remembering what's in which book. Each reading of her books teaches me more about teaching, creativity and how to find my own style and voice. Her fiction and nonfiction were the same, all there to teach me.

For my whole adult life I have taught beginning reading as I learned it from Ashton-Warner's books. I've used Key Vocabulary with hundreds of young children, in Harlem, in San Francisco and in Pasadena, in public and private schools, in childcare programs and in the charter school I founded. *All* the children learned to read and received honor from their families and peers. Like Sylvia I can say, "I know all this because I've done it."[2] At that time I knew nothing of Sylvia Ashton-Warner but *Teacher* and *Spinster*.

In 1985 I found Sylvia's autobiography, *I Passed This Way*, in a secondhand bookshop in Atlanta. I spent months reading this tome, trying to understand Sylvia's life and her insights, roaring with laughter at some of the stories, falling in love with Keith, shaking my fist at Sylvia's "Permanent Solid Block of Male Educational Hostility" and watching her families: the first, crazy, huge, disorderly one redeemed by Puppa and his stories, and the second, anchored by husband Keith and full of her own three children. I read the bits that seem cranky and babyish, and those that soared. I was intrigued. On the dust jacket of *I Passed This Way* was a list of all of Sylvia's published books.[3] Since Sylvia had died in 1984 there would be no more. In 1985-6, I read them all.

She wrote of adults and children. I found her fictional adult heroines, Germaine, Anna and Tarl, easy on themselves yet disciplined, visionary yet unpopular, sensual yet unfulfilled, awkward in society yet interesting. I was like that. So, I am sure, was Sylvia. Her women had passion for fairness, for work and for those they loved. They were trying to make bridges between the different cultures in their country as I was trying to make bridges in mine. Sylvia's writing helped me make sense of my struggles, my priorities. Twenty-five years after I first read Sylvia, one of my Pacific Oaks College students said it perfectly: "She reminds me of me."

NOTES TO CHAPTER ONE

1. *I Passed This Way*, page 324.

2. *Teacher*, page 32.

3. Except *O Children of the World!* Sylvia's songs and stories for children, published in Canada in 1974 by Dan Rubin in an edition of 1000, and *Stories from the River*, published posthumously in New Zealand.

4. *Myself*, page 26.

5. *Mana Waka is an extraordinary film* made by Merata Mita, a Maori woman, from 50-year-old silent footage. Mita used about 90% of the raw footage, and added a full sound track, including every hammer blow. The film tells the story of two ceremonial canoes built in the late 1930s at the behest of the Maori queen for a powerful spectrum of political, spiritual, economic and aesthetic reasons.

TWO—BREAKING DOWN AND REBUILDING:
SYLVIA'S LIFE INFORMED HER WORK
AND HER WORK INFORMED HER LIFE

Unless I am warm I cannot work, unless I work I cannot be well, unless I am well I cannot love and unless I love I do not live...whereas to live is the thing in a world at war, with slaughter the key word. [1]

EARLY CHILDHOOD:
"WHEN ALL THE CHANNELS WERE OPEN"

Sylvia Ashton Warner was born December 17, 1908, at Stratford, New Zealand. Her mother's teaching jobs took her large family to a succession of small towns and villages: fourteen during Sylvia's childhood. In the absence of lasting, constant community, each family member took on a disproportionate importance. Her mother, Margaret Maxwell, Sylvia described in her writings as large, overworked, snobbish, impatient, domineering and intimidating. Margaret taught in racially separate Maori schools to support the family. [2] The Warners were poor, often living on potatoes and porridge and jammed into a too-small house with outdoor plumbing, supplied as part of Mother's pay.

Sylvia's father, Francis Ashton Warner, [no hyphen here, Sylvia and her mother took on the hyphen well after Francis' death in 1926] was an imaginative, romantic, slight, severely crippled man, born in England. From the time Sylvia was born he stayed home and minded the babies. He told the children captivating stories. Sylvia was a middle child, sixth of the nine who lived, and given the name—Sylvia Ashton Warner—of a sister who died in infancy. The family apparently didn't make much of the Sylvia who lived. In her (adult) writing one sees little Sylvia experiencing ongoing satisfaction with painting and playing piano, very curious about her sexuality, and feeling frustrated that she received so little recognition. [3]

Toward the end of her life she recalled her childhood as "a time when all the channels were open." [4] She remembered roaming their rural communities with her two closest sisters, free to explore the mysteries of a large world. [5] There was a lot of work to do in that enormous, impoverished family, so the children generally felt safer away from home than in it, escaping a mother who kept the same school hours as her children, and on weekends and after school always grabbed the nearest child to do the next job. By age seven Sylvia had lost at least one important battle to her mother. She was naturally left-handed, but her mother pinned that sleeve behind her and made her use her right hand. [6] Since Mother was also Sylvia's schoolteacher until Sylvia was eleven, her round-the-clock impact on the child was profound: Sylvia escaped whenever she could.

Father was different. He took Sylvia's active imagination to faraway places and let her play in imagination with other little princesses. He was a poet-parent who gave form and legitimacy to Sylvia's inner life. He could trace his pedigree back to the fourteenth century, to a John le Warner who fought (on the losing side) in the Wars of the Roses. He also was the basic nurturer and cook of the family, and Sylvia writes repeated images of him stirring the porridge and the potatoes.

From notes she made later we learn that in childhood Sylvia was afraid in the dark, that she had some scary experience on the side of a cliff, that she was traumatized by earthquakes in a nearby city. Her active fantasy increased all her fears. The other children in her family teased her about her fears.[7]

As a child she could manage these fears because many outlets were available. She practiced piano, she listened to her father's stories, she drew pictures and swam and spent time with her sisters outdoors. So she met some of her needs to express and discharge her fears every day.

In the Wairarapa, a community which even today draws high school students from a vast, sparsely populated, sheep-raising area, Sylvia rode the long distance to high school on a horse and later on an old motorbike. She was a good student but had great difficulty socially. She was ashamed of her clothing and the squalor of her home. She posed and acted the way she thought people would like her to be. It was during high school that Sylvia's mother, her older sister Grace and Sylvia herself began hyphenating Ashton-Warner, to distinguish themselves from some lower-class Warners who weren't Ashton. In high school, Sylvia reports, she was "acting most of the time, before most people."[8] She yearned for romance with boys but "got nowhere" because they thought her ugly, and so she "retreated into phantasy." Graduating, Sylvia received awards for sports and art, and for an essay she wrote about Helen Keller.

YOUTH: THE SEARCH FOR LOVE AND FREEDOM

It was time to settle on a career, and for respectable poor women in the 1920s the only careers possible were teaching and nursing. Two of her sisters, Muriel and Daphne, became nurses. Like her sister Grace, Sylvia followed Mother's path and became a teacher, though she knew she wanted to be an artist. "No matter which way I wriggled and dodged, I couldn't get clear of the teaching."[9]

Sylvia's father died when she was seventeen, in 1925. She memorialized him as Puppa in *Greenstone,* the story-filled novel she wrote and rewrote for many years. From her writing he seems more a mythical character than one of fact and bone and flesh.

From 1928-31 she simultaneously attended Auckland Teachers College and Elam School of Art. By her college years, she reported, she was still nervous but had no identified fears. She explained that she was leading too interesting a life to give room to fear. She went up in an airplane, wore flapper clothing, was something of a party girl and speeded in cars, behaving irresponsibly and recklessly until an accident made her nervous in cars again. She found her sexuality awakening and others responding to her. Her boy-mad behavior interfered with her work, and she took deeper plunges into fantasy. Finally an unhappy love affair pointed out to her the "inadequacy of [her] present character."[10]

Unsatisfactory or not, her love affairs took her closer to marriage.

> I was still at the unsteady stage of not knowing whom I would marry and of course there was only one real unwavering goal for any girl who called herself a girl and that was Holy Matrimony, never mind careers or freedom or anything like that. In marriage all problems would solve themselves automatically; you'd be making love all night and all day too for which no doubt the man would recompense you by having your shoes resoled which were leaking half the time.[11]

She met Keith D. Henderson at the College in 1929. The courtship was full of romance:

> We kissed back the sweetness a little. The touching of lips said we were alive and were sitting side by side. "What I like, "he said, "is being together."[12]
> ... It was the kind of heart's climate that drew from me many paintings for K.D.H. which I would post to him. ... forty years later I found them among his things in his desk, romantic pictures of long-stemmed glasses of bubbling red wine which I'd never tasted, fantastic flowers and ladies and several impressions of city streets crowded with bustling people, encounters in Queen Street on Friday night, eyes of starry intent. Glances in passing. Vivid colours. And a picture of the wheels of a train grinding out from a station.[13]

Despite this extraordinary ardor, Keith kept her waiting, and more than two years elapsed between their first plan to marry and their wedding. Sylvia didn't like the waiting, but her writing shows her happy in this period, living for clandestine meetings in railway stations and hotels, for which both of them could have lost their teaching careers.

> Oh yes it was professionally unprofessional, deliciously risky, but no price was too high to be together even though paid for later. The only word in our vocabulary: together.[14]

Clearly, the only way to keep a man who was conventional to the core was to marry him, even though this would deny another inner voice which spoke insistently of independence and art. She put creative expression on hold, becoming instead a bride, a teacher and a dependent. Many years later, looking back on this period of courtship, she would name her crisis: "a clear-cut choice: love or freedom."[15]

Her notes tell us that just before her marriage she experienced herself as beautiful, and found her new personality highly successful in winning admiration and reciprocation. Sex realized was better than sex in fantasy. Her search for sexual fulfillment led to marriage.

> The only images housed in my mind were a man called Keith Henderson, a wedding ring on my finger to show the girls and a white wedding dress with a veil. I couldn't see through this picture of a wedding, not a yard beyond it or an inch either side. All powerful goals which had thrust me since I'd been born, all apprehension of being buried alive in the country once more, vaporised before this white picture which screened off the future like the sun in your eyes.[16]

On August 23, 1932, Sylvia, madly in love, married Keith, a minister's son, tall, dark, handsome and with eyes "a bewitching blue,"[17] one who "measured and weighed his words." He probably married her because she was exciting and dramatic. In the photographs in *I Passed This Way* and *Sylvia!*[18] she appears tense, slender, stylish, with patrician features and a generally sharp-edged face, while Keith has broad shoulders and a mild, relaxed look. "His voice is soft, without any edges."[19] Early in her marriage Sylvia's fears were less severe, but she was nervous in cars and in the dark. She had found with Keith an answer to her sexual longings: "No interest in other men. Satisfied with Keith."[20]

EARLY MARRIAGE: "THE BREEDING TIME"

In 1935 daughter Jasmine was born, in 1937 son Elliot was born, and in 1938 son Ashton arrived. Sylvia didn't teach from the time of her marriage until 1938. Since Ashton was born much later than he was expected, Keith had gone across the country to the school alone. Sylvia arrived in remote Horoera six weeks late to begin her teaching job. She brought her little baby into the classroom with her, sometimes teaching across him. She experienced serious communication problems, since she knew no Maori language and the children knew little English. Sylvia was nursing her baby but not eating.[21]

From July 1938 to 1941 Sylvia and Keith taught at Horoera School, about as far from urban centers as one could get in New Zealand's north island. To arrive in the community one had to cross two wild rivers, waiting for a low tide. She writes of fording the Orotua River (*Orotua* means hidden danger):

> ... slow deep water, muddy and treacherous. On its floor secret logs may have shifted position in the last high tide. A shudder in the buggy as the wheels hit one, the jolt as the horses jerked it over. Which child should I save if the traces broke, the shaft split, a wheel came off or one of the horses plunged free? Yet there did come a further shore once more, the horses straining up out of the water upon the blessed bank, but never would I cross these rivers again.[22]

There was no way out of Horoera but back across those rivers, so Sylvia must have felt cut off indeed. Because Ashton was a restless baby Sylvia and Keith slept apart so one of them could "have an unbroken night to support the other during the day." She writes of missing "time, energy and audience" for drawing or playing the piano, and only having a place for them in her dreams. Teaching cut into this dreaming. So did her loneliness for sophisticated city people and the artist's life.

They cut out an ad for a big car and pinned it up on the living room wall, planning to "rip up and down the North Island recovering the warmth of communication, kisses kisses all the way." The stresses were great, what with babies, work and having to travel far—and only when the tide was low—for all necessities.

Keith went away to a family wedding and was gone for nine days —at home the food ran out. When a Maori neighbor looked in and saw the problem, she returned on the next low tide with a platter of food. Sylvia was "becoming shy of the white people now, my children too maybe, and there remained another white visitor yet who was due some time and that was the school inspector." It was in this context, afraid of being judged inadequate, after little more than a year of teaching, and teaching ineffectually, that Sylvia broke down.

Teaching didn't go well. Not only was Sylvia a neophyte teacher, but her three preschoolers accompanied her to the classroom. The words in the reading books bothered Sylvia from the start and the children she taught seemed "bad," but she did not link these two problems. She could see that teaching Maori children to read in English made little sense, but that was her job. "What if we had a whole set of books with their favorite words or even words in Maori? They'd all read in no time."[23]

Creative work was a "frill" she never got to:

> ...now and again I won an hour on a Sunday afternoon, but although my piano work, like my drawing, wanted to burst out and soar among the rafters of a school room as it had since I'd first known I had fingers, there were some factors missing: time, energy and audience. Besides, these would not make me a better wife and mother or a better teacher either. The only place for them was in my dreaming.[24]

Sylvia couldn't manage both her own children and the school children at the school, so she set up a bedroom in the house to teach in and conducted her teaching there for a while. She managed to pass one inspection in this location with a good grade. Ambitious, she studied the Maori language and music from Keith's correspondence course books. But as her second year began she felt unable to teach even at home, and spent more and more time incapacitated, in bed.

What in the '40s was called sex drive had cost Sylvia dearly; unreliable birth control led to surprise pregnancies. Although she wrote in detail and at great length about her courtship and marriage, Sylvia disconcerts her reader by omitting all but the slightest reference, in her autobiographical work, to her pregnancies and childbearing.[25] In her sixties she said of her youth: "I stopped writing during the breeding time."[26]

Her autobiography first mentions her children thus: "Five years and two babies later I'm saying, 'I'm prepared to go teaching again.'" These two sudden babies are followed on the same page[27] by the mention of "the new baby coming." I think she writes little because she doesn't want us (or perhaps herself?) to see how overwhelmed she was by motherhood, and how angry. Nonetheless, her resentment seeps through:

... with three small babies we're out of circulation anyway. With two, we are. I haven't seen a racquet or a basketball or—or a film since...since...or had a swim or ...[28]

What a shock to discover yourself mothering three children under the age of five, a fate that threatens to transform you into someone like your own mother, your life governed and distorted by the sheer numbers of your dependents!

In Horoera Sylvia and Keith began sleeping apart and denying themselves sex because of "tiredness and unsatisfactory birth control."[29] As the mother of three unplanned children Sylvia was afraid to risk more.

The relationship with Keith changed:

He's grown bigger, broader of shoulder and heavier....His clothes speak protection to me as if they were part of his body. He pours the water in the teapot ...I fold a last nappie making a work of art of the pile for no one can fold nappies like me. I see him putting out the cups on the bench, his wide hands with strong knuckles which are gentle with cups and babies and a wife....He brings the tea and sits down.[30]

Teaching, marriage and motherhood paved a grievous path for Sylvia. Folding diapers expertly could only momentarily qualify as art. She was writing nothing, had no time to practice piano, was unable to paint and lived remote from the kind of discussion that sustained her. She was extremely unhappy and always acting.

She would later write about that period describing how she acted a part as a young wife: "I was a martyr and model of generosity to [people in the] district generally, to friends, at instigation of pride. Acted blitheness and inconsequence. Dropped acting before Keith."[31] The result of all this acting was that she was frantically unhappy, bewildered and suffocated by her own counterfeit behavior. Pressure built up. She couldn't drop acting before *herself.*

BREAKDOWN AND REBUILDING: "I'M NOT MUCH OF A CHARACTER"

By 1939, now thirty years old, she was unable to take care of her children, her teaching job, her home or herself. Local doctoring did nothing to help, nor did a stay with Anglican Mission Sisters in what she later described as a white room with white walls, white linens and white people, unlike the Polynesians she had become used to.[32] Slender to begin with, she lost so much weight during her illness that it imperiled her life.

Keith, who didn't go to the war because he was a teacher, boarded out the children and took Sylvia to Wellington, for treatment with Dr. Donald Allen, a psychologically sophisticated neurologist. Sylvia saw members of her original family at the hospital. She described the appearance of her sister Daphne, "her legs like twin poems." One morning:

> "How are you Sylv?"
> "I'm mad, Daph."
> "How do you know?"
> "I can't read and big black clouds keep rolling towards me from over that direction."
> "Why can't you read, Sylv?"
> "I can see the words one at a time and I know what they are but when I get to the next word I've forgotten what the first word was. So I can't read a sentence as a whole."[33]

Her brother and mother came. "There's nothing wrong with Sylvie ... she's quite lucid," her mother said, but her brother said, "She was dying of fear, Mumma."[34]

Sylvia's autobiography devotes a scant three pages to her interactions with Dr. Allen. As with other momentous events of her life, she lived it rather than wrote about it. But she wrote a chart for Dr. Allen describing what she thought had happened in her life. Here she mapped out her psychological history so that she and Dr. Allen could look at the conditions that were incapacitating her and devise measures to prevent it from ever repeating.

From the chart it seems clear that Sylvia's "breakdown" was precipitated by overwhelming anxiety. Keith went to be trained to serve in the war effort and Sylvia panicked. He went away to a family wedding and she was terrified.

Sylvia had made herself a bed she couldn't lie in. She was lost to her calling as an artist, unsafe without Keith's protection. She was stuck with her children, couldn't keep Keith close with the war summoning him and she saw no help out of her predicament.

By the time she got to Dr. Allen, anxiety had paralyzed her. She wrote: "Fear overpowering. Acute when Keith was away. Encroached on me in isolation at night. It developed when I was removed from Keith to the conviction of insanity. Religion no match for fear." After her first visit to Allen, the chart reports: "Fear at its worst—isolation nearly unbearable." Tucked into the box on the chart are the words, "longed for death."

Allen understood this anxiety and depression as arising from Sylvia's growing loss of authenticity. He appears to have gone directly to this issue. The chart pays close attention to Sylvia's compulsive "acting," to her insistent presentation of false selves to provide the children and the community with the perfect teacher, wife and mother they expected.

Inauthenticity plagued women of my generation too, young wives in middle-class urban America in the 1960s, who remember with some shame how we acted out roles meant to satisfy the community's expectations as well as our own vision of what a proper wife and mother should be. This vision was built of images from television, literature and our own childhood memories and fantasies. For most of us it took another twenty years—well into our forties—to learn to listen to the inner voice which would help us determine how we truly wanted and needed to live our lives. Sylvia felt all of the pressures we felt, and had the additional burden of living in an outpost of the British Empire, expected to do one's duty and conceal one's emotions. Astonishingly, it was in conventional, dutiful New Zealand that Sylvia Ashton-Warner began a life-long habit of listening to her inner voice, embarking on her journey toward abundant life in 1940!

After Sylvia's first visit to Allen the chart reports:

> Unsuccessful effort to overturn acting—firstly at your (Allen's) advocation—later, seeing the distance between my assumed self and my own self, for shame. But it stuck from a lifetime's habit.

Allen's method of fostering Sylvia's authenticity was straightforward. He led her to talk about forbidden things: her fantasies, her sexuality, her fear, the real facts of her relationships with people, the importance to her of art and music, the conditions under which she was able to work.

She learned that attending to her creative work made rest possible: "Need for comfort brings book to head again." Her final entry about fear: "Access to people and association with Maoris[35] and visit to you with consequent greater understanding of dealing with fear, greatly diminished fear. Seeing cure of fear in expression helps progress of book." Maori culture encourages the immediate and full expression of deep feelings. If Sylvia hadn't been exposed to Maori culture, we might never have heard of her.

Allen was especially tough on Sylvia in the area of her fantasies. She seems to have fantasized compulsively about sex, fame, power, romance and happiness. He regarded this activity as a substitute for real creativity and an avoidance of reality. "Your dreaming," he tells her, "is just common theft."[36] Sylvia's chart documents the growth of this tendency from childhood. It shows her attempts during her therapy to separate fantasy from reality in order to use her imaginative forces in the service of her creativity.

Everyone who knew Sylvia agrees with her own assessment that the images welling up inside her demanded passionate expression. Allen taught her that these images were based in "the two great powers in the personality which qualify all living: fear and sex."[37] At this period there was no "appropriate" outlet for her sexual love or her deep fear, and that lack caused her illness. Sylvia's strong need to assert her uniqueness—a need unmet in her childhood—extended into her later life. When Allen met her she had abandoned all her channels for asserting her uniqueness, and Allen responded to that loss, insisting that she reconstruct them.

Perhaps his most important service to her, and indirectly to all the teachers that Sylvia later influenced, was Allen's explanation of why Sylvia could not read. He showed her how, when she was choked with unexpressed images, she couldn't take in any more ideas. She would come to understand that a child who is full of news, confusion, rage or wonder must express it before he or she can attend to the teacher's lesson. Her inability to learn from books and the inability of young children to learn from books came from the same source. As the therapy progressed she regained not only the ability to read, but to write as well.

After calling her dreams theft, Allen asked Sylvia what she was, and she said artist, wife and mother. He challenged her:

"Why don't you answer you're a teacher?"

"I forgot."

"You mean you don't want to teach other people but to get away in a corner and do it yourself?"

All too true.

"Do you *want* to know what you are?"

Nothing.

"You're a writer."

I look away from him and tell the blue curtains, "Well I might have been if..."

"Don't say *if;* it's the weakest word in the language."

I don't think Doctor likes me so I tell the blue carpet, "I tell you what I'm not, Dr. Allen. I can see for myself that I'm not much of a character."

This time he doesn't answer curtly but looks out between the curtains rather wistfully to the city, turning over a pen in his fingers reflectively. "Maybe humility would be as good a base to build on as anything else. To rebuild on." [38]

Here we see Sylvia momentarily shed, in the safety of Allen's supportive presence, the dreaming and role-playing that had plagued her. For this moment all the roles were stripped away, leaving her to look directly at herself. And she was ready to hear her doctor.

Allen knew Sylvia needed to express what was inside her. She was gifted in many ways, and could have painted, sculpted, played music, danced or acted on the stage to express her imagery. Fortunately for us, he chose to tell her to write.

After several weeks of this work Sylvia returned home by train and horse with Keith, crossed the frightening rivers, and resumed life with him and their children. Sylvia now perceived clearly that her daily functioning and her life were at risk if she stifled her expression as an artist. Keith came to believe this too, and from then on, he gave Sylvia the time and freedom necessary to pursue her arts. Her readers find Keith refreshing and romantic, making sacrifices in the name of love. I have heard more than a few people say Keith was a saint. Some New Zealanders said that Keith was embarrassed by Sylvia's behavior, but I have found no evidence to support that. Rather, from the time of the breakdown forward, Keith graciously supplied to Sylvia regular, frequent times when he would tend the children and do the cooking, the gardening and the washing, so she could go to her study and work. As Sylvia wrote, Keith was the mother of the family, with Sylvia another of his children. People who knew him report that this nurturing brought Keith gratification. Apparently he also enjoyed, while remaining in the safety of his own unblemished respectability, Sylvia's flouting of convention.

Did Dr. Allen, in those intense weeks, "cure" Sylvia? She never broke down again, was never again immobilized by fear and the clogging that came from not expressing herself. She went on to develop teaching methods based largely on what she had learned about the human psyche from Allen, supplemented by her varied reading. She was remarkably productive: writing, playing piano, drawing and painting. At age 51 her first book, winnowed from thousands of pages of journals written in the previous decades, was published. She became famous all over the world.

But working with Allen did not make her perfect, nor did it free Sylvia from pain. She was never able to surrender her "acting," which often took bizarre and grandiose forms. To the extent that Sylvia's rebuilding included overblown, inauthentic characterizations, Allen's treatment was a failure. She was awkward, rude, inappropriate, anguished in her interactions with people much of the time. On balance, however, it seems that from the time of this therapy onward she possessed the resources and methods necessary for productive survival, if not for joy.

We mustn't make an icon of Sylvia, herself an iconoclast. We learn from her *because*—although she was flawed and difficult—she was able to grow and produce. What she learned about coping she used as a teacher, and that is what good teachers *do*. From experiencing, confronting, understanding and overcoming a major life crisis, Sylvia learned to organize her life for survival. Her life as a teacher was similarly impacted; what worked for her—expressing herself, sharing herself, taking time for herself, heeding her inner voice and relinquishing conformity—also worked with the children.

The following chapters show Sylvia using this learning with the children she I believe that every teacher can learn from Sylvia this extension of the personal into the professional. What finally, did Sylvia get from her therapy? Rumer Godden contrasts two characters in her novel, *A Candle for St. Jude:*

> *She had tried to be the things she felt she should be: gentle, considerate, unselfish, patient and as truthful as she could and, yet, she had little of life while Madame, who was wilful, inconsiderate, passionate, and not always strictly truthful, had life in abundance.*

Like Madame, Sylvia managed to have life in abundance.

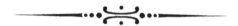

NOTES TO CHAPTER TWO

1. *Myself,* page 147.

2. Reading between her daughter's lines I gather that Mother Warner probably wasn't a very good teacher. She was certificated and snobbish, but didn't teach in white schools. At this time most teachers in Maori schools were uncertificated, almost all were Pakeha. She would have earned considerably more money teaching in a Pakeha school. [See glossary of Maori words.]

3. Many of the pictures of Sylvia's life before 30 come from a chart of her personality she made for a neurologist at about age 30, which can be found in the Ashton-Warner collection at Mugar Library. (See Chapter Ten for more about this chart.) Other stories of Sylvia's early life come from *I Passed This Way,* her autobiography. Less reliable, because it is more fictionalized, but shelved in most libraries with the autobiography, is *Myself,* a memoir she wrote in her fifties, about her life in her twenties.

4. Shallcrass interview. (See Appendix I, Chronology, 1975.)

5. Shallcrass interview.

6. I imagine her at five or six, left sleeve pinned behind her, clenching both fists and promising herself: "when I grow up *nobody* will tell me how to do *anything!*" There were interesting outcomes to the changing over of her dominant hand. People who knew her have told me that Sylvia could draw two different pictures with her two hands, simultaneously, and could write a sentence on the chalkboard with both hands working at once, starting from the two ends and finishing neatly in the middle.

7. From the chart explained in note 3, above.

8. From the chart explained in note 3, above.

9. *I Passed This Way,* page 216.

10. From the chart explained in note 3, above.

11. *I Passed This Way,* page 190.

12. *I Passed This Way,* page 230.

13. *I Passed This Way,* page 214.

14. *I Passed This Way,* page 212.

15. *I Passed This Way,* page 216.

16. *I Passed This Way,* page 234.

17. *I Passed This Way,* page 228.

18. A 1988 biography by Lynley Hood, Viking, New Zealand.

19. *I Passed This Way,* page 188.

20. From the chart explained in note 3, above.

21. This section summarizes what Sylvia tells us of this period in *I Passed This Way,* pages 244-270.

22. *I Passed This Way,* page 257.

23. *I Passed This Way,* page 264.

24. *I Passed This Way,* page 264.

25. She also omitted writing about her father's death.

26. Shallcrass Interview.

27. *I Passed This Way*, page 244.
28. *I Passed This Way*, page 245.
29. From the chart explained in note 3, above.
30. *I Passed This Way*, pages 246-7.
31. From the chart explained in note 3, above.
32. *I Passed This Way*, page 278.
33. *I Passed This Way*, page 280.
34. *I Passed This Way*, page 280.
35. Maori people have long rituals which bring focused community attention to grief. This is in contrast to English (or Pakeha) people who value reserved behavior instead.
36. *I Passed This Way*, page 282.
37. *I Passed This Way*, page 281.
38. *I Passed This Way*, page 282.

John and Peter started off.

Soon John saw something.

"Look, Peter," he said.

"There is a new green ball.

Janet had a new green ball."

John picked up the ball.

"She has been there," said Peter.

"But she has gone away."

John and Peter went on again.

A page from the *Janet & John* readers Sylvia found
in her classroom.

THREE—MAKING THE CLASSROOM PEACEFUL THROUGH ARTISTIC EXPRESSION: SYLVIA DEFUSES WHAT SHE CALLED "THE IMPULSE TO KILL"

The only time they show any sign of interest is when I let them draw, when it seems that furtively they let escape the pictures rampant in the mind—these pictures in the mind that offend so, that disorganize real teaching. If only their black heads had nothing whatever in them, then all I would have to do is fill them up. Empty children couldn't be naughty. Or when I tell them a story. They attend to me and sit wonderfully still. It seems then that their minds and my mind become one thing, two friends arm in arm.[1]

At age 29, with two children and one more on the way, Sylvia became sure that she wanted something more in her life. She had taught very little since she had become credentialed to teach.[2] First the Great Depression made teaching positions scarce, and later her marriage interrupted her career. Now she urged Keith to leave the Pakeha (white) school system, and teach in the Native Schools Department, the only place a married couple could teach together. Their first position was in a particularly remote area, where "you couldn't distinguish between the rhythm of your soul and the rock of the rolling ocean for the sea didn't sleep but wave-crashed your mind and took over."[3]

Nothing in her training as a teacher had prepared Sylvia to be a major influence on resourceful, ingenious Maori children. At Auckland Teacher's Training College and Elam School of Art, Sylvia had been taught to conduct a proper primary classroom with the focus on the teacher: to write a clear plan of what is to be learned, then to hold recitation and make sure the plan is covered thoroughly. The power of the teacher over the child formed the subtle background for teacher training then, as it still does in many—perhaps most—places around the world. Sylvia didn't feel competent:

> Perhaps I care too much about the appearance of the thing. They all look so nice, and the room looks so nice with its generous areas of color. But with my increasing study in the early morning I am more and more inclined to wonder if it looks as nice inside. All the books I study are about the *inside.* I should know more about the inside and I have picked up a bit. When I'm teaching formal number and reading I'm well aware that the children are concerned with something else, or some

of them are. If only I came across some passage in a book about how to relate the outside to the inside when at work teaching children; there was a book at training college about that very thing, Rousseau, I think. [4]

During Sylvia's early teaching, in the late 1930s and early 1940s, she saw that if she taught Maori children as she had been trained to do, they didn't learn her lessons.

"Jacob, have you finished your work?"
"Please no."
"Tiny has. Look, all that." I held up Tiny's exercise.
"Please she copied it off ... off—" glancing about him experimentally—"off Whitu."
"Please I didn't," from Tiny. "Please I copied it out of myself."
"Jacob, bring me your exercise book. Let me see it."
"Please I ... please it's not here."
"Where is it?'
"Please at home."
"I told you not to take your book home. You'll have to go home and get it. Up you get ... off! Go home and get your book."
"Please I can't."
"You've got legs."
"Please yes. But the canoe it's not there."
"What's the canoe got to do with it?"
"My grandfather took it."
"Where?"
"Please he took our canoe downriver to the other pa because there's a tangi there because a man got drowned last night. He was eeling."
"What have *eels* got to do with your exercise book?"
Tiny beside me, who is truly tiny like a little black beetle, said, "Please Jacob he live on the other side of the river. He comes to school in the canoe."
"Am I to believe that a boy of Jacob's size goes to and fro across that wide deep river in a canoe every day?"
"Please my big sisters bring me. They in Mr. Hen'son's room." [5]

Sylvia ponders on this revelation:

" ... they're not thinking about what they're writing about or about what I'm teaching. I'm teaching about 'bed' and 'can' but they were thinking about canoes and grandfathers and drowned men and eels. It seems to me ... I seem so *rude to intrude....*"

Keith responds: "That's just it. Well, dear, that's what we're paid to do, just that: intrude."[6]

Intrusion was a violent act, an act expected of teachers. What could she use in its place? In desperation she experimented, following Jacob's lead, and told a story about canoes, grandfathers, drowned men, eels and the children. Then:

Glancing down upon Jacob's tears I know I have not intruded, that I have fraternized with him. I see in his large brown upturned eyes the potential of a good boy.... A boy you could lead into being what a boy should be, through affection; wanting to do what you wanted. A boy in whom all things are possible. But life goes on, teaching goes on and reading goes on and a teacher herself must obey the curriculum. My grading will be very bad if they can't read their books and I'll be called a poor teacher. As the children get out their reading books and I go to the blackboard here is the bed and the can again and all about I can jump. As my chalk rebels a moment, a flash of insight comes: I'm turning Jacob into a naughty boy.[7]

This homicidal intrusion of one upon the other—that's what my teaching is most of the time, especially the reading, intrusion upon their inner thoughts and feelings, but *I* do it every day, every school hour of every school day, and it's the pain that makes them naughty.[8]

From close observation of children Sylvia learned that she didn't get anywhere "pasting on foreign material." Sylvia saw the necessity of moving toward the children's angers, hurts and fears:

I suppose they still give them books about the birds in the trees and the breeze and all that, thinking that by giving them peaceful books they'll make the children peaceful. But what they're doing is fragmenting them further, disintegrating them. The thing to do ...is to give them bad books like themselves, then you'd integrate them, then you'd get them peaceful.[9]

In an interview for New Zealand Television at the very end of her life, Sylvia recalls:

> I spent my life studying in the undermind of our child, to learn and understand the instincts and impulses, because I wanted to isolate the impulse to kill. I wanted to isolate it and to find out how I could harness it.[10]

What she needed to learn was the psychology and the culture of the children, so that her material wouldn't be foreign and her lessons wouldn't violate the children. She studied the Maori language and learned what she could of Maori history.

Maori people first came around 800-900 AD in ocean-going canoes from Polynesia to the land they named Aotearoa, which signifies "The land of the long white cloud" and was later named New Zealand by the Dutch. Each canoe carried dozens of people across many hundreds of miles of open sea. In the late 18th and early 19th centuries, before British settlers took over the ownership and government of the land and marginalized the Maori, they made wonderful works of art. Their carving embellished their war canoes, meeting houses, weapons, ornaments and containers. Beautiful flax-weaving told important stories, as did the painting of rafter patterns. Ceremonial cloaks were splendid, distinguished and ornate, some decorated with geometric borders, others with thousands of feathers.

Maori ceremonies included, and still include, a remarkable level of ritual speechmaking for welcomings, partings and, most of all, during the substantial time Maori people spend expressing their grief. They also had highly complex chants and action songs (*haka* and *waiata)* and shell, bone and wooden musical instruments which they played tunefully and skillfully. Since the Maori had no written language, their educational system involved face-to-face apprenticeships which ordered and preserved these arts.

Elders taught children their history through having them memorize genealogical chants which went back beyond the Polynesian canoes to the beginning of the world. This oral tradition demanded deep concentration and developed remarkable memories, as well as requiring systems of substantial interpersonal interaction between generations. Roles within the community were fitted to people's abilities and disabilities, their ages, their genders and their talents.

Victorian colonization forced most of the Maori arts and some of the action songs underground—especially the erotic songs. The missionaries replaced traditional children's culture with book learning in schools whose focus was on learning to read, speak English and give right answers rather than on becoming connected to tribal history, culture and arts.

The Europeans who colonized Aotearoa saw Maori people enjoying all those pleasures—immediate gratification, expression of violent or sexual feelings, preference for the arts over other work—which "civilized" New Zealanders of European background were eager to suppress. The missionaries designed schooling for Maori children, intended to "correct" this cultural difference. Colonial schooling brought to the fore the children's best and strongest defenses, so Pakeha teachers, including Sylvia's mother and Sylvia herself at the start of her teaching, often experienced Maori children as unteachable and wild.

By the 20th century most Maori parents used English to communicate with their children in the belief that this would help them succeed in the dominant culture. Maori leaders today view this decision as a serious mistake, since it nearly cost them their language. From the 1840s to the 1920s it had been generally expected by Pakeha New Zealand that the Maori and their culture would die out. But the Maori were made of sturdier stuff and, in increasing numbers, claimed a fair share of the rich land which had once been wholly theirs. Maori meeting houses and greeting ceremonies, Maori carving and flax-weaving, and Maori songs and chants—in fact all aspects of Maori culture—are much more widespread today than in the late nineteen-thirties and early -forties, when Sylvia and Keith taught in remote communities in the separate government-run Native Schools Department.[11]

As she was recovering, she tried to make use of her new learning from Dr. Allen, and also attempted to make sense of her classroom. To this end, she and Keith both studied the Maori language and gained some proficiency in it. Keith also made frequent visits to gatherings on Maori tribal land.[12]

The Maori children Sylvia taught were caught squarely between two cultures, two languages, two value systems. What finally made Sylvia's work with the children effective was the artist in her communicating with the artist in them. To the extent that all were artists, the cultural gap was small. She had learned from Dr. Allen that she couldn't take in new images when she herself couldn't read.

Sylvia and Keith taught children who learned *te reo* (the Maori language) in their homes, and were expected to learn their English in school. Her writing about this problem still is useful for teachers teaching across culture—she was uncomfortable with introducing reading in a foreign tongue. In *Greenstone* Sylvia lyrically helps us see the Maori people struggling to rise and regain some power over their land.

In 1943 Sir Herbert Read's ideas would reform and revolutionize Sylvia's attitudes about teaching. His *Education Through Art* is said to have altered the balance of the education system in Great Britain,[13] and it caused a big stir in the New Zealand Schools Department. Read was a Renaissance man: a distinguished art critic, an anarchist who became a knight, a prolific writer and a psychologist who translated the works of Jung.

She read the education department's new scheme based on Read's ideas about art education and took inservice training on the subject from the Department of Education art supervisor. For once in her life, doing what she was supposed to do rewarded Sylvia richly:

> *Education Through Art...so* answered every question I'd ever asked myself that I sent to London for the book to study it and didn't put it down for about ten years.[14]

Read's books showed Sylvia the connection between art and a workable classroom. What comes out of the child—likely strong feelings—will be grounded if it comes out through art.[15]

In his monograph on Read, James Collinge, of Victoria University, Wellington, cites only "a few isolated cases" where, as Read wished, "art has...permeated the entire fabric of education." These were the cases of Sylvia Ashton-Warner, Elwyn Richardson and Sybil Marshall. We can learn from their examples.

Marshall's books, *An Experiment in Education*[16] and *Adventures in Creative Education,*[17] describe, as *Teacher* does, a lone teacher during the war years reinventing her classroom so it will serve children well. Marshall calls her method "symphonic" and combines a vision of childhood creativity with practical, teacherly advice.

Richardson's *In the Early World,*[18] tells about teaching six- to thirteen-year-old Maori children, with a central emphasis on the arts. Children of this age group are more interested in products than younger, process-oriented children. So, given the opportunity to create, Richardson's primary school children made magnificent crafts and artwork, poetry and plays, and many of their images illustrate his book. Richardson paid close attention to fostering the children's ability to discuss work with each other respectfully and critically. In February, 1990, Richardson told me that at the time of publication he had been advised, "Your book will not be as widely read if you specify that the children are Maori." In a 1990 interview, Richardson told me he regrets following this advice, omitting mention of the ethnicity of the children. As we see by this example, New Zealand education history is entangled at every stage with the perceptions Maoris and Pakehas have of each other.

Sylvia studied Read's writing, and strove to implement his theory in her work. Fifteen years after Sylvia discovered Read, Read discovered Sylvia. In 1958 he wrote an enthusiastic introduction to *Spinster:*

> ...this book, however unprofessional or un-academic it may seem, is a book of fundamental sig-nificance. Without exaggeration it may be said that the author has discovered a way of saving humanity from self-destruction. We should not ignore her method because it is so unassuming, so unpretentious. Great changes in

the destiny of mankind can be effected only in the minds of little children.[19]

Before fame arrived, Sylvia was alone with the driving force of her own internal imagery. Bolstered and challenged by Read's writing, she thought about what that imagery might mean in teaching. Dr. Allen had recommended that she write, to release space in her mind. Now she began to experiment with making similar space in the minds of the little artists she was supposed to teach. This idea organized her work. Although the reading books supplied by the school system were sterile and frustrating, the children's own stories and passions gave her human material to work with. *Seeing the children as fellow artists* helped her abandon colonial attitudes toward them.

She wrote (based on what she'd learned from Read, from Tolstoy, from Erich Fromm and from Dr. Allen) that *the* antidote to destructiveness is the creative expression of what moves us.

While her reputation is based on her method of teaching young children to read, and on her other humane and imaginative ways of being a teacher, Sylvia often declared that all of her work was in the service of the search for peace, in particular, the search for ways to "defuse the impulse to kill."

To a visiting, perhaps apocryphal, teacher who confided "once you've got your foot on their neck they're all right,"[20] she explained:

> The volcanic energy, precipitated from the combustion of the old race and the young, the volcanic energy of the New Race blows—but is directed. It was exhausting at first, this controlling of the direction of the blasts; and not without risks, this changing of the vents, for the young Maori warriors are full of 'take, break, fight, and be first' when they come; but it is not as exhausting or as dangerous as standing in the way of it.[21]

Sylvia knew this metaphor: she *was* the volcano. Her breakdown and subsequent psychotherapy had convinced her, once and for all, that she must pay attention to the creative monster living inside or it would destroy her.

The phrase "education for peace" joins Read and Sylvia. In 1949 Read wrote that physical expression in labor or art is necessary to avert war.[22] In 1966 Read said, "Art is the name that we give to the only human activity that can establish a universal order in all we do and make, in thought and in imagination. Education through art is education for peace."[23]

Read validated Sylvia's style of thinking, in images. He said children think in images and can use imagery to work through their pain. As she read Read she formed her belief that effective teaching supplies a moral alternative to rage, a creative answer:

I can't dissociate the activity in an infant room[24] from peace and war. So often I have seen the destructive vent, beneath an onslaught of creativity, dry up under my eyes. Especially with the warlike Maori five-year-olds who pass through my hands in hundreds, arriving with no other thought in their heads other than to take, break, fight and be first. With no opportunity for creativity they may well develop, as they did in the past, with fighting as their ideal of life. Yet all this can be expelled through the creative vent, and the more violent the boy the more I see that he creates, and when he kicks the others with his big boots, treads on fingers on the mat, hits another over the head with a piece of wood or throws a stone, I put clay in his hands, or chalk. He can create bombs if he likes or draw my house in flame, but it is the creative vent that is widening all the time and the destructive one atrophying, however it may look to the contrary. And anyway I have always been more afraid of the weapon unspoken than of the one on a blackboard.

With all this in mind therefore I try to bring as many facets of teaching into the creative vent as possible, with emphasis on reading and writing...It's just as easy for a teacher, who gives a child a brush and lets him paint, to give him a pencil and let him write, and to let him pass his story to the next one to read.[25]

She observed how fascinated the children were with each other: "If only they'd stop talking to each other, playing with each other, fighting with each other and loving each other. This unseemly and unlawful communication!"[26] So she had the children read to each other and hear each other's work.

Struggling with her inadequacy and her incompetence in her early teaching, Sylvia developed several *dispositions*[27] which would hold her in good stead in her development of appropriate *curriculum* for children. As we explore these dispositions below, please note a consistent theme. In each disposition Sylvia begins by acknowledging and allowing the presence of tension, energy and potential destructiveness, and only then does she lead the children toward order and peacefulness.

OFFER MANY CREATIVE OUTLETS

The first disposition was to make sure that children were offered expressive outlets, like those she offered to herself. Sylvia noticed the children had experimental interest in representing and making things: "The way they draw bombers and make them with anything and roar around the room with them."[28] She built more and more time for making and doing into the school day, to let this energy out.[29] She learned to understand that wiggling children needed time for a walk, or a dance, or a story. The children's behavior changed in direct response to expanded opportunities to express themselves in art and other media. Our children today need to be told a different story to counter the violence, rashness, dependency and sneakiness that television teaches. They must learn that superheroes can't be relied upon to swoop down and solve our problems, but instead, each of us has enough strength and art to solve them, with the help of our friends.

Throughout her writing Sylvia bellyaches, groans, fusses and moans about being a teacher, but nowhere in her writing, published or not, do we find her complaining about being an artist—in fact, she writes of the artist's life as the very best one, with madness as one possibility but fame and sexual fulfillment the other:

> ... brilliance of imagery may carry an artist off into another world, a lonely and fearful world in which we are cut off from the mainstream of reality. We hear other voices speaking and see other faces; another life altogether flashes. Asylums are full of people whose brilliant imagery has carried them off forever and famous tombs are full of those who managed to get back over the border with their booty. The physical life, the bodily touch, the real fleshed union is the way back over the border....[30]

Because Sylvia preferred art to teaching, her energy was well spent when she could finally remove reading—or any other required school subject—from the *teaching* category and reconsider how to share it as an *art.* Then she could deal with questions which have many answers, each answer provoking interest in the images of the artist, in place of questions with only one, correct, conversation-stopping answer. Against all of the schoolteacherly traditions of her culture, she envisioned and then instituted in her class a first-thing-in-the-morning output period when anxieties and violence could be brought to the surface and defused. She discovered that with the teacher using what has surfaced as the text, children can learn more naturally.[31]

Her sensitivity led her to want harmony between her program and the children's concerns. Empathy was the current which carried her. Recalling her own childhood, she wrote of identifying early with others:

> Not exactly a clinical compassion but an innate disposition to *become* other people ... their feeling became my feeling contagiously, their strapping my strapping, their pain mine and I couldn't do anything about it.[32]

TEACH WHAT EMERGES FROM THE CHILDREN. OTHERWISE YOUR TEACHING WILL BE INTRUSIVE AND DO THEM VIOLENCE

A second disposition was to avoid intrusion and other violences which adults can mete out to the children who are in their power. Sylvia used her own analysis and intuition to find a way to teach in harmony with the children, in place of received methods of teaching or what she called "homicidal intrusion." Remarkably, she listened to her insight and refused to turn children for whom all things are possible into naughty boys and girls. Integration of children's passionate interests with her own responsibility to teach them English and reading solved the problem of intrusion. Reading Tolstoy, Sylvia learned that "Art, and art only can cause violence to be set aside."

In her autobiography, her memoirs and her fiction she documented her search for appropriate educational strategies. Her novel *Spinster* shows Anna, the teacher-heroine, searching for clues to an unforced, graceful way to bring Maori children to English reading:

> Sometimes when I am working late at night over my Maori reading books I almost see this key. Sometimes I think it has traffic with violence. The colours make me think that. They make me think of the passions in their homes, in their ways, and tucked in alongside of the gentleness.[33]

Sylvia came—dangerously but inevitably—to believe in a curriculum driven by children's interests as well as her own. After frogs had been seen at the pond down the road they became the center of interest: "Frogs infiltrated the number lessons and injected the reading lessons so that Satan scored a victory."[34]

Why does Satan figure in a story of what we have come to call *emergent curriculum*? I believe that letting non-prescribed elements into the curriculum is to this day perceived by many teachers as unholy, perfidious, a reason for exclusion from the club. The frogs were a tool of Satan, then, because they broke the pattern the teacher was meant to impose.

She carefully scrutinized the materials she was given:

> To write peaceful reading books and put them in an infant room is not the way to peace. They don't even scratch the surface ...[35]

The matter of "bad" books became a central early childhood education controversy in 1963 (certainly not for the first time) when Maurice Sendak's book, *Where the Wild Things Are*, was first published. This fantasy dream book, whose wild-child hero goes virtually unpunished ("and there was his supper waiting for him, and it was still hot") made many adults uncomfortable and even angry, while children, even today, ask for it again and again. The triumph of the story occurs when Max becomes the autonomous and powerful king of all wild things: "And the wild things cried 'We'll eat you up we love you so.' And Max said 'No!'" Max's autonomy, which leads to adventure and the love of the strange and huge Wild Things is very different from earlier children's books where the wicked are punished and the good rewarded. We have learned from the children's response to *Wild Things* that they all know they are Max, usually wicked and barely skirting trouble.

In a more recent book, *Daddy is a Monster Sometimes* (Harper and Row, 1980), John Steptoe shows Daddy growing fangs and losing his temper when the children push him too far. This happens in the book as it does in real families, after the umpteenth diversion at bedtime or when the children take second ice cream cones from a stranger who misinterprets and embarrasses their daddy. This book frees children to talk about how frightening it is when adults are angry and to begin noticing their own anger as something normal and human. And in *Noisy Nora* by Rosemary Wells (Dial Books for Young Readers, 1973), the heroine, who is being paid less attention than she wishes, does very bad things like dropping her sister's marbles and flying her brother's kite downstairs, and ultimately disappears, whereupon her family searches for her and grieves for her and finally appreciates her as she deserves.

Sylvia would have adored these "bad" books! She cared about facing one's feelings squarely: one Saturday in isolated Pipiriki, during the enormously creative period when she wrote the journals which became *Myself, Greenstone,* and "Rangatira,"[36] she went to her study and drew abstract pictures of four people, including herself, "in the metaphor of the ground." Describing the picture of her own spirit she says:

> ...a black cavern full of ravaging flames with no surface coverage at all ...I realise I have at last learnt ...to peel off sentimentality however sore the process, to escape from the representational and to speak in uncluttered symbol.[37]

So she wrote her own bad books for the children—in uncluttered symbol—always about relationship, and found the children learned their skills, now that she taught about what interested them.

AVOID CULTURAL IMPERIALISM

A third disposition was to avoid cultural imperialism. Maori people had their ways of doing things, and Sylvia spent a good bit of time listening to her Maori children, thinking about how to work with them. She had always enjoyed differences and listened for them. She determined early to build a bridge between the cultures, enriching herself in the process. She learned to ask rather than to assume. Somehow it wasn't difficult for Sylvia to see Maori people as individuals with talents and interests she could engage.

Sylvia suspected that it made the rural Maori violent when she tried to teach them to read using suburban English *Janet and John,* the assigned reading book.

> " *...*have you seen a train, Ihaka?" "No Mrs. Hender-son." "Well, that picture is of a train. People have a ride in it. It goes by itself like a truck but it isn't a truck. It's like a long long mail car with a lot of seats and it makes a very big noise and it can carry fifty people. The mail car can't carry fifty people. And it doesn't go on the road because it has its own road, all to itself. See that word beside it? That word is 'train.' Can you say 'train'?" "Train," from [Ihaka]. "T-r-a-i-n. Spell it like that." He does, clearly. "Now I'll see if you can write it." "I can't write it." "You might be able to. You bring me your blackboard and chalk and duster." But he remains where he is. ...
>
> A shame. With his twice-daily trips across the river in Grampitty's canoe he should be trying to write "canoe," but when [he has] his things he sits on the floor at my feet and says unexpectedly, "I can write train," and the next thing he has written quite a good word except that it is not "train." What is this word? I look closer. It is "canoe." Then he forgets all about me and draws a canoe with the family sitting in it.[38]

Here Sylvia conjures up a story about how she was teaching "train" while Ihaka was learning "canoe." Her fantasy helps her avoid the impossible choice between violating the child's culture or her employer's. This surreal story depicts her longing to reconcile what she perceives to be respectable teaching with what she perceives to be authentic, culturally salient learning. She tells it brazenly, as if it were what actually happened, relieving herself of the colonial burden and showing us the way.

Her ability to unify the things she was learning into good curriculum—to implement those practices which grew out of these three relatively new dispositions—expanded markedly once a number of conditions changed in Sylvia's life. By the time she wrote the journal entries which became *Spinster* and *Teacher,* she had put into use many particulars learned in her therapy with Dr. Allen; her youngest child was well out of babyhood; and Keith was firmly committed to giving her time to study. Her work room, the Selah, was ready. Her neighbor and beloved friend Joy Alley was interested in her work and cared about her.

While she never would achieve integration of her personality or inner calm, by this point she had learned how to struggle with her issues and survive. Though she didn't have the perseverance and stability to teach well for sustained periods of years, she had learned enough to help thousands upon thousands of teachers teach well—into an extremely distant future.

Why is culturally salient teaching and learning so often threatening? Perhaps because what comes to the surface isn't always respectable. Sylvia ran a risky course letting repressed material emerge in New Zealand, a country she said still had "a crinoline over its head." Sylvia's observations of the children as she heeded these new dispositions combined with theory from Read and others and gave form to her teaching precepts:

> "Touch the true voice of feeling and it will create its own vocabulary and style," its own power and peace.[39]
>
> Supply the conditions where life comes in the door: let it.
>
> Supply the conditions where the native, inborn imagery of our child can surface under its own power to be captioned or named, harnessed, put to work and to make its contribution to society.
>
> Supply the conditions where the impulse to kill can surface to be isolated and defused.[40]

In the '60s and '70s I used Sylvia's lessons on the importance of acknowledging and harnessing children's passions in order to free them. This helped me toward harmony in my classroom. With frequent key vocabulary lessons and daily access to paints, clay, dancing, sand, water, dramatic play and blocks, the children I taught became more supportive and kinder to each other over the course of the school year.

I wasn't the only teacher who used Sylvia's vision on the way to my own. She had a deep, widespread influence on the movement toward integrating cognitive and affective learning. The "educational romantics" of the sixties in the United States, including Paul Goodman, Beatrice and Ronald Gross, John Holt, Herbert Kohl and Jonathan Kozol; the progressive early childhood educators, including Asa Hilliard at San Francisco State, Elizabeth Jones at Pacific Oaks College, Claudia Lewis at Bank Street College and Polly Greenberg with the Mississippi Child

Development Group; courageous reading specialists, notably Jeannette Veatch and Katie Johnson, read her, quoted her, assigned *Teacher* to their students and built parts of their theories upon her contributions. Their writings agree that as teachers, caregivers and parents, we create good learning environments only when we learn ways to base our work upon children's social interests and creative capacities as Sylvia taught us to do.

Children burst into classrooms each morning with news: good news, bad news, but always news important to the bearer. Whether this is received as material of significance or as bothersome childish twaddle makes all the difference in the world in math, in English, and most of all in social studies. When the teacher requires the child to stifle this material because the teacher has more important things to teach, the child loses some respect for the teaching-learning process. If this happens often enough, the child decides that learning is another name for oppression, and resists mightily, often making violent attempts to get even. When, instead, the teacher listens and uses the classroom as a laboratory for processing the news, amplifying it when it's wonderful or grounding it when it's shocking, the child learns that learning is purposeful and supportive, giving life and energy. People who know how to learn and want to learn are the ones who can think about making peace.

Sylvia contributed to peace: first in her classroom and later in her writing. She meant to do so in the great world, as well. In 1954 she wrote an article which was published in *Here and Now,* a magazine Sylvia's sister Evadne perceived as pro-communist. Sylvia wrote a scathing letter to Evadne which reveals more of her political view than any other document I have found:

> I was appalled to have an answer to my letter commending to you the paper Here and Now as I'm not used to answers to my letters...receiving your reply, warm, well-argued and defensive, roused long-forgotten uncomfortable sensations of pleasure...
>
> From your letter it is apparent that I left somewhere in your apartment an impression that I was pro-Russian, pro-communist and pro-enemy. ...The truth is that you have underestimated me. I'm far worse than pro-Russian, pro-communist and pro-enemy. I'm much more dangerous than that. I am pro- my sons.
>
> I'm enclosing my elder son's target paper at 25 yards. Now in some obscure and reprehensible way this precision of his in shooting which he learns at school makes me curious about the enemy whose heart one day may take the place of this cardboard. Try though I will to be a good New Zealander and have no interchange with the enemy, still I find myself wondering about this other

heart and whether it is half black and half red and has rings on it round the bull's eye. God knows I have learnt that to be interested in the enemy who may one day practise the steadiness of hand and eye on your own sons is most un-New Zealand; while the eye-shut technique, the one-minded press and the precision bullet-work is the thing. Nevertheless along with Eisenhower, Churchill and Stalin, I have contracted this disgraceful habit of peering under curtains whether iron nylon or mutton to see what this enemy is like. I just can't stop wondering if their hearts and cities will make as good targets for my sons as these exciting rings on cardboard. No I just can't.

Then there is this incorrigible taste of the artist for the truth. If only we could leave it alone. If only I could contest this dreadful habit of questioning the rule of the wd. And what a disastrous susceptibility to boredom grows from being brought up among interesting people. If only I could enjoy the bleating repeating press....If only I could stop reading papers from outside New Zealand from older countries and from nations with different ethics and from countries without the lapping of a surrounding sea. If only I could unpossess myself of this agogness about bull's eyes and rings on the hearts of the enemy.

You reject *Here and Now* because "you think it might have a red tinge." You're quite right to reject it. You'd better reject me too. Because I'm interested in even worse than a red tinge. I like the bright red papers of the reds themselves. It was only when I found the communist revealing himself as he really is in his own writing in his own papers that I found out for myself what he is....Give me the bright colour itself to find out the quality of the pigment. God knows I realise how disgraceful and un-New Zealand it is to admit to having held a red paper in my hand. But there's a limit to the resistance against temptation and the essay, five pages long, that I read in a copy of a Chinese publication recently outlining exactly what Chinese writers were to write, and how, I found so fascinating a revelation that I at once fell into my un-New Zealand tendencies of wondering and thinking beyond the mutton curtain: wondering about trivialities like freedom of the mind and of the spirit. Yes I actually was. I was wondering if perhaps I am behind in my vocabulary and that freedom had changed its meaning since I last read Shelley; wondering what it would be like to have to compose your hero to a stated pattern, instill in him pre-arranged

views, describe him in prescribed terms and to.. to.. But
there's no telling what mothers will do when they see
their sons in uniform making good scores at target
practise.

As a matter of fact, Evadne, the paper *Here and
Now,* with or without the red tinge, is even worse than
you suspect. It's a forum. It's a place where you can
discuss openly anything from iron to nylon and mutton.
Openly mind you. And this wretched disposition it has to
turn things over so that the underside shows and the way
it peeps under curtains. You can even talk about targets
for sons. I made a mistake alright in commending it to
you. And you were dead right to reject it. If only I could
remember how to apologise I would.

Oh to be a worthy New Zealander. Oh to stop
turning things up on both sides; to stop looking beyond
and beneath the press; to resist eavesdropping by curtains
and above all to stop wondering what this enemy is like
that my sons may meet some day. Ah dangerous mothers
of sons...

In 1970, just after Keith's death, Sylvia traveled half-way around
the world to set up a peace school for Rotary International "in the
Hebrew University in Jerusalem with the children of the lecturers as
pupils."[41] This came to nothing because she left Israel to be with her son
Elliot in England when he became seriously ill just a few weeks after
Sylvia's arrival in Tel Aviv.[42] When that crisis was over, another—the
death of her daughter Jasmine's husband—called Sylvia back to New
Zealand.[43]

What led Sylvia to think of peace as a curricular goal? All teachers
of young children experience conflict as it arises among the children or
between what the adult wishes and what the children are willing to do.
Sylvia looked closely at conflict. Besides, she taught cross-culturally, and
the Maori children were far more fierce in their expression than was
comfortable for her. Also, she had seen World War II and
felt—resonating with her fear of intruding upon children—the fear of
possible Japanese invasion. She had experienced for herself the value of
the arts in reducing her own anxiety and anger, and saw the arts
practiced by Maori people, who have a tradition saturated with creative
arts. Using creative outlets wouldn't be "pasting on foreign stuff."

I have come to believe that to bring about this curriculum of peace
we adults need to learn to become comfortable thinking and feeling
together with children about death, about pain, about divorce, about
meanness—when these matters arise, and they will. It is not possible,
nor would it be a good thing if it were, to teach only the rational, the
sweet and the soft. Liberated teachers are as comfortable with
feelings—including divergent feelings—as with thinking, including

divergent thinking. Our human minds and hearts work best together and worst when ruled by passion alone or by intellect alone.

Comprehensive arts education provides an opportunity for integrating feelings—including angry, painful and violent feelings—with thoughts. This integration is necessary if we want to become honest, modest and respectful people, struggling for equilibrium and fairness and learning to value the journey. Sylvia wrote:

> Do you too aim to be a worthwhile person or only a worthwhile teacher? How do you see teaching—as a source of income or as a work of global status? I wonder if you'll think, when you read through this, that I was moving in the right direction—if you will think as I did then that war and peace might...only might...be in our hands, conceived in the early years of children, the classroom the incubator. Or will you think I was wrong?[44]

NOTES TO CHAPTER THREE

1. *Myself,* page 35.

2. Sylvia did teach at Eastern Hutt School for one winter term—a few months—early in 1932.

3. *I Passed This Way,* page 258.

4. *Myself,* page 67.

5. *Myself,* pages 21-22.

6. *Myself,* page 23.

7. *Myself,* pages 25-6.

8. *Myself,* page 100.

9. *Myself,* page 110.

10. Endeavour TV, *Sylvia Ashton-Warner.* National Film Library, Wellington, 1977. Interview with Jack Shallcrass.

11. Today Pakeha New Zealanders no longer expect the Maori people to die out, but instead some have begun to see Maori culture and language as entitled to a place of respect in the country. Toward that goal the first bilingual class in Aotearoa (New Zealand) was established in 1977, and in 1987 Maori was made an official language, alongside English. Today the greatest hope of the Maori people for their cultural survival is in a new (1980's) institution, the *Kohanga Reo* (language nest)—a system of preschools where native Maori speakers, generally women of the grandmother generation, teach young children their language and culture.

12. The couple were affiliated with Maori schools until Keith died. Apparently Keith preferred them since he wanted Sylvia with him and liked the autonomy he found in that system. The appointments were, initially, easy to get:

> Maori schools were . . . under . . . the administration of the Native Schools
> department which called for special qualifications; music was one and art was
> another. We both had music and I had art so we were firmly and officially
> appointed.   —*I Passed This Way,* page 247

Sylvia worked in Maori schools until *Spinster* came out in England in 1958, when she stopped teaching full time. But her connections with the children in the school did not end then. As headmaster's wife she arranged gala musical productions and taught individual and choral music, culminating in major community recitals. Keith gained and kept unusual high respect from the Maori community, so much so that he was given, in addition to his Pakeha funeral, a Maori one at the Judah marae, (traditional, sacred land) where his casket was covered with a ceremonial feathered cloak.

13. H. Moore, "A Tribute," in *Herbert Read: A Memorial Symposium.* R. Skelton, ed. Methuen, London, 1970.

14. *I Passed This Way,* page 329.

15. In New Zealand in 1990 I inquired widely about the effect of Read's work on classroom teachers, given the publicity his work received there in 1946-7. Of those I asked, only Elwyn Richardson, author of *In the Early World* (see bibliography) seemed to feel a debt to Read. Apparently the normally iconoclastic Sylvia was one of a very few teachers who took her department's espousal of Read's work seriously.

16. Cambridge University Press, 1968, England.

17. Oxford, Pergamon Press, 1968.

18. Pantheon, 1964.

19. Sylvia met Read once. Sir Herbert and Lady Margaret Read stayed with the Hendersons and then motored with them from Tauranga to Wellington in 1963. Since there is nothing to be found in the writings of either on the subject, I gather that their one meeting was an anticlimax.

20. *Teacher*, page 102.

21. *Teacher*, page 105.

22. I believe...that the aggressive impulses of the peasant are discharged against a permanent enemy which we generally call 'Nature.' The struggle against weather, against erosion, against weeds, is a struggle which fully engages whatever death instincts the average human being is endowed with. Anyone who spends long days hoeing sugar beets, slashing hedges, or mowing thistles has little taste for the bayonet. I know that the Englishman who shoots grouse or pheasants, or hunts the fox, is often a fierce and blood-thirsty militarist. But he is not the peasant: it is not the peasant who follows the hounds, but the idle gentry, the retired businessmen. The peasant has no leisure for such pursuits: his sadism is fully satisfied in a day-to-day struggle with the earth. . .

An ingrained sense of what one might call Mother Earth gives to the peasant a sense of security which is unknown to the city-dweller, whose existence depends on a cash nexus. City-dwellers, and the industrial proletariat in general, live under the fear of economic fluctuations—slumps which mean unemployment and his social outcasting. The peasant may suffer from fluctuations of prosperity, due to drought or storm; but these are disasters which spur him to further activity, to renewed aggression against the elements. The unemployed proletariat have no natural outlet for their aggressive impulses, and are therefore, as Hitler found, ever predisposed for war.(pages 26-7)

I think we might risk the generalization that wars are always made by idle people—meaning by 'idle' people those not engaged in active muscular work. . . .(page 28) We are not secure in our pacifism unless our aggressive impulses are fully engaged elsewhere—in life-promoting activities, in life-protecting activities, or merely in mock-destructive activities like sport. It is not a *moral* equivalent for war that we need, but a *physical* equivalent, and it should, of course, be the aim of education and upbringing to give us just such an equivalent. . . .(page 29)

I believe that nothing less than a complete recasting or reorientation of our educational system can promote peace, can save mankind from annihilating wars. But what is needed cannot be covered by the timid approaches of the average educational reformer. Reform means that you take existing elements and shuffle them into a more satisfactory pattern: you revise the curriculum, raise the school age, build new schools. But that is not what I mean: I mean a complete transformation of the methods and aims of education. . . .(page 34)

Education must be through arts, through gymnastics, through creative play of all kinds; it must be under the patronage of Dionysus rather than Apollo, and it must project, into physical celebrations, into dramatic fantasies, the aggressive impulses which are latent within us all. From this point of view the phenomenon of *catharsis*, the purgation of the emotions recognized by the Greeks as taking place in their drama, takes on a clearer significance: catharsis is precisely a discharge of aggressive impulses, and particularly of the death instinct, through imaginative participation in tragic events. —*Education for Peace.*

23. Lewis, 1966.

24. A New Zealand "infant room" is an entering class of five-year-olds.

25. *Teacher*, pages 93-5.

26. *Teacher*, page 103.

27. Thanks to Lilian Katz for unearthing this most useful word.

28. *Teacher*, page 104.

29. The importance of representation in early education is still being uncovered, especially in the work going on in the Italian city of Reggio Emilia, where the arts-based public municipal childcare system is working effectively and with great beauty. The reader is encouraged to study *The Hundred Languages of Children*, the catalog of a remarkable exhibit of children's work from Reggio Emilia which has been shown in Europe and the United States. Another very useful book on the Reggio approach is Lilian Katz and Bernard Cesarone's *Reflections on the Reggio Emilia Approach*, published in 1994 by ERIC-ECE. A third resource, by Carolyn Edwards et al, also called *The Hundred Languages of Children*, was published in 1993 by Ablex (see Bibliography).

30. *Incense to Idols*, page 189.

31. *Myself*, pages 168 and 234-5.

32. *I Passed This Way*, page 47.

33. *Spinster*, page 61.

34. *Myself*, page 169.

35. *Teacher*, page 96.

36. This last was published by Hodder and Stoughton in 1986 as part of *Stories from the River*.

37. *I Passed This Way*, page 309.

38. *Myself*, pages 85-6.

39. Partial quote from Mary Coleridge.

40. *I Passed This Way*, page 354.

41. *I Passed This Way*, page 384.

42. This sojourn in England resulted in a novel, *Three*, a thinly veiled and dreary novelization of Sylvia's life in 1969, about a son in the hospital, his wife, and his mother.

43. *I Passed This Way*, page 384.

44. *Myself*, page 11.

FOUR—NAMING THE PICTURES IN OUR HEARTS:
CONTEMPORARY APPLICATIONS OF
THE KEY VOCABULARY[1]

The primary word is not a straightforward symbol for a concept but rather an image, a picture, a mental sketch of a concept, a short tale about it—indeed, a small work of art.
　　　—Lev Vygotsky[2]

I miss my daddy.
　　　—The most powerful "word" in my first grade class, 1994

In her early years of teaching, Sylvia found it baffling that the Maori children—quick and expressive in their conversation, their play, and in learning what interested them—were achingly slow at learning to read. The education establishment knew this too.[3] She wrote:

> The reading books I found there for the primers that first Monday morning began with four nouns on the first page: horse, bed, train and can, briefly illustrated. Horse they could understand as nearly all of them rode to school along the beach or from over the range, but a train they had not even heard of. Some of them had beds at home but some slept on the floor or the earth while a can was straight-out enigma to all; the sketch showed one of those little watering-cans you see stitched in fancywork on old-time tea-cozies which I hadn't seen myself for decades. On the second page, regardless of having used the can as a noun, it suddenly became a verb: I can skip, I can run and such. "It's a funny thing, K, but I can't teach some of the little Maoris to read."
> "It's using that noun as a verb," he says.
> "But they don't know what a can is anyway, or a bed or a train."[4]

Sylvia struggled for years with the simple question, Why don't these bright children learn to read? Her training didn't prepare her to answer this productively, but her own differences from the Pakeha mainstream did: Like Maori people she preferred art to rational discourse, the dramatic to the prosaic, and sensory vitality to Victorian prudery. She also noted, as Harold Taylor wrote, "The direction of learning is from emotion to thought to expression in words, symbols or symbolic action of some kind—not the reverse, as most educators think."[5] How could she harness their passions to help her children read?

Sylvia studied in books and in her classroom. Now that she was alert to psychological workings, "the undermind," she observed the children and their creative outpourings in new ways. In the book she valued most, *Education through Art*, she was taken with Herbert Read's discussion of the child's ability—still present in some adults—to see a clear picture in the mind's eye of events, people and things not present. Read, a Jungian, was intellectually rooted in Plato. He taught that discipline is embedded in the arts, and that children would become disciplined from the inside out if they were educated through the arts. All of this got Sylvia thinking. She was able to use what she had established with Dr. Allen about basic human drives in understanding her schoolchildren. Fear and sex, the impulse to kill and the impulse to love, were driving them, too. Like her, they were full of stuff which, unless expressed, blocked intake of anything new.

Combining Read and Freud's ideas, Sylvia gave each child reading words that named that child's own passions, anxieties, interests and fascinations. Her respect for each child's unique imagery was central to her work:

> Imagery is the source of action. The first concern
> of a teacher is to address himself to the *NATIVE* imagery
> of our child and see that it remains alive.[6]

As she experimented, she discovered that the children became avid and fluent readers when each child read words selected to evoke the pictures of the beings and objects foremost in his or her heart. Since she was trying to stop intruding upon children, she now tried instead to follow their lead, finding their reading vocabulary in their own stories. She would later formulate the introductory work with Key Words:

> *First words must have an intense meaning.*
> *First words must be already part of the dynamic life.*
> *First books must be made of the stuff of the child*
> *himself, whatever and wherever the child.*[7]

Thus, Ihaka, a little boy in New Zealand in 1940, would read his words—*ghost, mummy, kiss*—depicting the strongest imagery in his mind. And Cynthia, a little girl I taught in San Francisco in 1980, would read her words—*monster, mommy, hot*—depicting the strongest imagery in hers. The words would unlock the children, freeing them to take in new imagery. Because they opened doors Sylvia would come to call these words *Key Words* or *Key Vocabulary.* Both of these terms describe the first stage in a process Sylvia called Organic Reading.[8]

Where was this Key Vocabulary to be found?

> I reach a hand into the mind of the child, bring out
> a handful of the stuff I find there, and use that as our first
> working material. Whether it is good or bad stuff, violent
> or placid stuff, coloured or dun. To effect an unbroken

beginning. And in this dynamic material, within the familiarity and security of it, the Maori finds that words have intense meaning to him, from which cannot help but arise a love of reading....[9]

How does this procedure work? Paul Goodman wrote:

> ...Consider...the method employed by Sylvia Ashton-Warner in teaching little Maoris. She gets them to ask for their own words, the particular gut-word of fear, lust, or despair that is obsessing the child that day; this is written for him on strong cardboard; he learns it instantaneously and never forgets it; and soon he has an exciting, if odd, vocabulary. From the beginning, writing is by demand, practical, magical; and of course it is simply an extension of speech—it is the best and strongest speech, as writing should be. What is read is what somebody is importantly trying to tell.[10]

At a very early lesson, Sylvia sat with her pupil, the Maori child Rosemary, and conversed with her. Sylvia listened until she heard something from that layer of Rosemary's mind or heart which had a distinctive resonance, carried an electrical charge, made a bell ring. Then Rosemary might speak up: "I want *ghost.*" Or she might wait until Sylvia offered: "You were talking about a fierce ghost. What word would you like?" She would pause, and if no answer came, continue, "Shall I write *ghost* for you?"

When teacher and child agreed on it, *ghost* was her new word. If they didn't agree they would search further, together. Sylvia kept assessing Rosemary's connection to the words, helping her know her own strong feelings. When they found a Key Word Sylvia printed it on a large card and gave it to Rosemary, holding the child's finger and tracing the letters with it, naming the letters and having Rosemary repeat them. Later that day Sylvia would pour all the new words of the children out on the floor. Each would claim his or her own word, and tell the others something about why it was special. The next day Rosemary would easily read *ghost* if, indeed, it was the right name for the image in her heart. After playing this game a few times Rosemary would often arrive at her lesson, ready with a new word. If Sylvia agreed that this word was Key, she'd write it down on a card for Rosemary. If Sylvia was unsure, they'd discuss the word until they reached some agreement. Sometimes Rosemary's mother or uncle would come to the classroom and hear her words. Sylvia encouraged family members to make themselves at home in her classroom, probably because she knew enough about Maori culture to understand that what was valued by the extended family (*whanau*) would be important to the child. She made books of these wonderful words, and children took them home.

If Rosemary didn't remember her word the next day, Sylvia would help her rid herself of it, saying, "Go throw this one away. I didn't give you the right one." And Rosemary would toss the word, having no use for it. The emphasis stayed on giving Rosemary reading words of clear value to Rosemary.

Some adults think throwing her word away might shame a child, but that isn't the experience of those of us who have taught using Key Vocabulary. Children happily get rid of what they don't need, as long as the adult doesn't grieve over the loss.

Often, at the beach, I collect seashells, and I rarely remember to bring a container. So I keep upgrading the shells in my hands, with little regret over those I return to the beach. I know I can't possibly have them all, so I want to keep the prettiest, the most interesting, the ones that seem to go together. Just in this way, the collection of definitely, positively known, deeply meaningful Key Words grows, and the child becomes a beginning reader.

After Rosemary knew the game and liked being a reader, Sylvia used Key Words with phonetic similarities (*monster, mustard, mama*) to help her understand phonetic regularities (*m* says "mmmm") and went on to use these words as a starting place for making up stories and books for Rosemary to read. Often in my class at Burnett School[11] children collected words that named people—family members and later friends and classmates—as their first Key Words. I'd ask, "How do you feel about your mama?" Cynthia would answer, "I love her." So I'd offer to add the verb *loves* to Cynthia's words. If she accepted, we'd stack the nouns on either side of the verb, read the sentences, and then I'd make her a book:

> *Cynthia loves mama*
> *mama loves Cynthia*
> *Cynthia loves daddy*
> *monster loves hot sauce*
> *daddy loves baby*

After a few books like this one children are ready for easy commercial story books, and are really truly Organic Readers. Rosemary liked going to Key Vocabulary lessons with Sylvia and Cynthia liked going to them with me because the lessons helped them feel more in tune with life. Your troubles are somehow lighter when you name them, and your triumphs are brighter when you proclaim them. Just as the toddler bursts into speech because representing experience through words is powerful and interesting, young children who study Key Vocabulary burst into reading, craving the written symbol (another level of representation of experience) for its power and magic.

Sylvia ran a risky course letting repressed material emerge in Victorian-feeling New Zealand. Here is some firsthand testimony on that subject, from Arthur Fieldhouse, Professor of Education at Victoria

University, Wellington, who visited Fernhill School in 1951 and observed Sylvia's teaching:[12]

> Professor [Collin] Bailey and I used to go up to Hawkes Bay for Inspector [Rowland] Lewis every year to do a week's course for teachers. One year he said he was very concerned about a scheme for the teaching of reading that seemed to be having wonderful results and there [were] some aspects that he was worried about and would we mind going out to the school to have a look.
>
> We asked what the problems were but he said he didn't want "to prejudice you. I just want you to see and make up your own minds." We didn't know about Ashton-Warner but funnily enough I had been seeing articles in National Education over the pseudonym Sylvia....I kept referring to these as they were a practical application of what I was saying...which was already established in the American literature. Sylvia Ashton-Warner was really translating it into practical terms. We went to the two-teacher school—98% Maori. There was a great buzz of activity going on but it was a meaningful buzz—you can always tell the difference between the meaningful buzz and the riotous one. We were introduced to her and she behaved most strangely. She took off into a corner of the room and we were left there abandoned, Rollo, Collin and I. They were lovely children. They were involved in reading and they came up and wanted to read to you, but my hat! what they were reading would rock you. This was really what Rollo was frightened of. That *Truth Magazine* or one of the newspapers would get hold of this. It was all the gossip of the *pa* [Maori enclave]. They could read like mad. I was a bit suspicious and wondered whether it was just learned off by rote. I isolated the words but they knew them all. It was incredible. It was in a sense very heartening. It was hard and fast proof that the theory works.

Lynley Hood quotes Professor Bailey[13] who tells about the same visit:

> It was the intensity of life in the classroom that appealed to us...Those little Maoris could read like mad. Their stories were full of violence and four-letter words, which seemed to be what Rowland Lewis was concerned about ... But it seemed to us that the colourful words

were part of the youngsters' natural expressiveness which she was anxious to nourish...We told Rowland Lewis that the basic principles of her work were sound, that she was tapping the most dynamic source of real teaching—the child's own life—and that it was worth taking the risk to encourage her...I recall [telling her] quite strongly that no reading books published in advance, and lacking the immediacy of the children's freshly remembered experiences and feelings, could take the place of her own method.

Many teachers have read *Teacher* or *Spinster* and tried to do Key Vocabulary. Since neither book is a manual, one must interpret Sylvia, and procedures may become distorted. The proper test of any variation is whether it supports the connection of the written symbol with the picture behind the child's eyes. For example, I keep each child's words in an envelope. Some teachers keep the word cards on rings. There's nothing wrong with either system if the cards are shuffled before a new lesson. The purpose of using separate cards is that each word tells a whole story of its own. The danger of memorizing a sequence of words is that the powerful impact of the Key Words will be diluted—the stories will be lost—and children will come to see reading as deciphering rather than as a way to take power over their lives.

Teachers who draw or glue pictures on the card or have children do so don't understand the primacy of the inner image. Sylvia has convinced me that this is crucial:

> Children have two visions, the inner and the outer. Of the two the inner vision is brighter. I hear that in other infant rooms widespread illustration is used to introduce the reading vocabulary to a five-year-old, a vocabulary chosen by adult educationists. I use pictures, too, to introduce the reading vocabulary, but they are pictures of the inner vision and the captions are chosen by the children themselves...the outer, adult-chosen pictures can be meaningful and delightful to children; but it is the captions of the mind pictures that have the power and the light. For whereas the illustrations perceived by the outer eye cannot be other than interesting, the illustrations seen by the inner eye are organic, and it is the captioning of these that I call the 'Key Vocabulary.'[14]

The word cards must contain only this powerful new symbol, not even a drawing made by the child. Why not? Look at the picture in your mind evoked by the word *mother*. Did you see your own mother? Can you draw her as clearly as you see her? Your picture—what Sylvia calls *the caption of the inner vision*—is located within you, and sometimes comes with smells and tastes and other sensations. Not even your own illustration of it will do the whole task of showing your mother.

So, if the child wants to draw, give her paper and let her go at it, and label the picture if she wants you to. That's fine. But keep the Key Vocabulary card plain. Any outer picture interferes with her inner vision and its word, standing alone, unadorned.

Another variation used by Jeannette Veatch (and the many who have learned Key Vocabulary from her) is to take words from children in a group, not one-to-one as Sylvia did. I speculate that taking Key Vocabulary in a group works to the extent that the teacher's and children's culture is the same.[15] Children who speak the (literal or metaphorical) language of the teacher can better resist copying and becoming inauthentic in a group. But where the child comes from a different community, the teacher, to provide a bridge, must learn the child's language, and to do this the teacher must meet alone with the child. My own preference is to meet one-to-one because I enjoy getting to know the individual children I teach.

Where children are culturally different from the teacher, from the administrators, from the curriculum committee or from the school board members, teaching children by using their own personal material will avoid cultural imperialism. This is basic to any movement for education which liberates and empowers learners.

I worked, one child at a time, with urban, highly stimulated four-year-olds, and later sixes and sevens, all in contrast to Sylvia's rural fives. In the urban setting, especially with the younger children, I ventured another variation on Sylvia's work. I asked children to close their eyes, in order to screen out distractions, and to take my hand, in order to feel safe with eyes closed. To elicit key words I began by asking pointed questions: "Whom do you love?" "What's the scariest thing in the world?" "What would you like to have in your pocket?" Sooner or later all of the children caught on to the game and came to me already knowing what word they wanted. This understanding of self comes with maturity. Some fours know their minds when we meet them, some sixes and sevens may need help.

Veatch also makes a point of *never* rejecting the word the child suggests. I disagree. The teacher is an active member of the search. Veatch quite correctly says the teacher "stirs up the child's inner cauldron." In my view the teacher looks for nouns that evoke vivid images. She takes responsibility if a word is chosen by mistake, and so she does her best to avoid mistakes by adding her insights to those of the child. She is the wise coach, not just the scribe, teaching self-knowledge as well as reading. If the child looks around the room and says he wants *table* the teacher can respectfully remind him of his passions: "Well, I could give you *table* but I could also give you *motorcycle* or *ice cream* or *Batman.*" This helps him to learn the game.

But this collaboration does not mean that the child asks for *horsey* and the teacher, thinking she knows better, says, "No, you like to fly airplanes. I'm going to give you *airplane*." Rather, the two must search for a mutually satisfactory word each time, and the teacher must bow to the inescapable truth that each of us is an expert about herself or himself, graciously believing that the child must make the final decision. When the child chooses the key word her face lights up and she stands taller.

The complicated, sometimes refractory part of teaching Key Vocabulary is identifying the Key Word. As you get to know a child this becomes easier. Observe Matthew when you get a free minute. Who is Matthew? What does he do when he's making choices? Does he choose to build with blocks or does he choose to do whatever Charles and Leon do? Is he close friends with Charles? Does he wish he were? *Charles* is probably a key word. If they symbolize competence and strength for Matthew, *blocks* will be a key word too. So is *Leon*, the name of the child Charles plays with instead of Matthew—this time the word is made key through jealousy, not through love.

It takes a close and trusting relationship between teacher and child for these searches to move along well. Keatsy was very angry one day when I asked him to come to his lesson. I had put him on the bench for practicing a karate kick on another little boy and though he still seemed angry, he came to me quite willingly, for his reading. I offered him *angry, bench* and *kick,* but he brushed all aside, and then said, in a definite, no-nonsense way, "I want *ice cream*." He used the reading lesson to move away from his pain, not into it. Of course, *ice cream* was a one-look word and Keatsy never forgot it, not even for a second. When children paint a picture at the easel it sometimes helps them heal, and we know nothing of the whole matter. So it can be with Key Vocabulary.

I have taught Sylvia's reading process to college and graduate students and working teachers. As they practiced taking Key Vocabulary from each other, these adult students asked for general words like *faith* and *trust,* but when we dug deeper, trying to figure out what pictures they represent, we ended up with *God* as the Key Word. They told me they wanted *busy* and *rushed,* but when we pursued the discussion I found they were getting married next month and the name of the beloved emerged. Then they lit up with a special glow, the way Cynthia did when she got *perfume* or *grandma*. Images are particular and concrete, not general and abstract. Searching together for images is a fine way to get to know each other.

In view of the widespread dissatisfaction with the results of American reading instruction we must look at any way of teaching reading that produces good results. *Look-say* instruction doesn't harness emotions: it leaves most children cold, uninvolved with reading except as it pleases the teacher. It was look-say that didn't work with Sylvia's Maori children.

Phonics doesn't work well in English: all of our vowels are multi-voiced and virtually all our orthographic rules have exceptions. Preoperational five- and six-year-olds aren't primed or prepared to recombine buh, uh and tuh, to get *but*. Despite this, many children are still taught to read in English using a graded set of basal readers, some of them very much like the *Janet and John* books Sylvia used to so little avail.

But is Key Vocabulary as good at teaching reading as the look-say or phonics methods? In 1971 the Vancouver Project, directed by Selma Wassermann, Sylvia's friend and champion at Simon Fraser University, measured the reading skill of children taught with Key Vocabulary against children taught in traditional ways. When the children were measured—on standardized tests which assume basal reading instruction—the Vancouver Project found no significant differences in skills acquisition but some large differences, favoring the use of Key Vocabulary, in children's attitudes toward reading. The quantitative data bore out the following conclusions:

> 1. Primary grade children who are introduced to reading through the Key Vocabulary approach tend to do as well on reading achievement tests as those taught in other ways, over a two-year period of time.
> 2. Children who learn to read by the Key Vocabulary approach, in the context of the "Organic Day" program, show significantly more favorable attitudes towards reading than do the matched control group.
> 3. Student teachers trained in these "laboratory" classrooms are able to implement "Organic Day" programs in their own teaching with considerable confidence.
> 4. All of the experimental children, without exception, learned to read. [16] [17]

The teacher who wants to use Key Vocabulary but faces resistance from the institution in which she works may want to use the Vancouver Project findings as support. The chart on the next page is a set of responses from one of the Vancouver Project schools to the item, "When I have to read, I..." on the Boning Incomplete Sentence Test.

The move toward Whole Language (though it is defined differently every place it is practiced), seems to be on the right track: It assumes that the words we want are in books which interest us, so that is where we should encounter them; that language has rhythm which isn't distorted by such books; and that writing shouldn't be driven by spelling. All these ideas can work best after we begin with Key Vocabulary, which introduces children to reading about themselves, their passions, their favorite people, places, and things, and their monsters. The link between Sylvia Ashton-Warner and Whole Language is meaning. Finding the child's first words in his or her heart insures that the text is chock-full of meaning.

EXPERIMENTAL	CONTROL
feel happy	read with my eyes
I like reading the whole book	read quietly
read it to the teacher	read nice
read it carefully	read when my mother tells
feel mad	read with my eyes
feel happy	read with my eye
am glad to read	read
feel happy	read with my eye
feel okay	with my eyes
happy	read with my eyes
feel happy	read quietly
feel happy	read
feel sad	read with my eyes
I say good	will read
feel happy	read science books
read to my friend and my auntie	take a book
read a book	read with my eyes
feel good	I don't like it
am very happy	read in my mind
read and when I finish I think of the story	
am sad because sometimes I didn't know a word	
get my book and read	

It is worthwhile to compare Sylvia's work with Key Vocabulary to the literacy work of Paulo Freire, who taught rural Brazilian adults to read using words that had political, environmental, and cultural significance. A good introduction to Freire's work is Cynthia Brown's essay, "Literacy in Thirty Hours." Brown describes the pictures and the techniques used by Freire to elicit discussion and the vocabularies he used to teach beginning reading. These differed from village to village, reflecting local conditions. Brown writes:

Freire and his colleagues developed the linguistic materials for their literacy program from two premises:

(1) Adults can learn to read with ease words that are highly familiar and meaningful to them. (2) It ought to be possible to select a brief list of words that would contain all the phonemes in Portuguese, so that learning this minimal linguistic universe would enable a reader to sound out any other words or to record any words he knew orally. (This premise appeared possible because Portuguese is for the most part a phonetic, syllabic language.)

...Freire's teams visited the community to investigate its culture. They explained why they had come and solicited help from volunteers from the community, whom they called coinvestigators. Together they examined all the familiar activities of the community, cross-checking their perceptions and analyzing the significant words used by the community.

...Teams prepared a picture to illustrate each word. For example, for the word *tijolo* (brick) a picture of a construction scene was prepared. This picture was shown first without the word *tijolo*. Only after the group had discussed building with bricks, their own houses, housing as a community problem, obstacles to better housing and whatever other topics were generated, was the second picture introduced showing the construction scene together with the word *tijolo*. In the third picture or slide the word *tijolo* appeared alone.

Teaching adults, Freire and his teams found these important images to be political and cultural. Here is a list used in one urban slum: brick, vote, crab, straw, odd job, ashes, illness, fountain, (sewing) machine, employment, sugar mill, swamp, land (soil), hoe, class. In a city on the sea, the list was: brick, vote, wedding, cart, fish, fishing boat, (fish) scale, Brazil, (sewing) machine, flour, coconut, hunger, food, union, work, cleanliness.[18]

The 1987 book *Doing Words*, by Katie Johnson, brings Ashton-Warner's work into the very end of the twentieth century, showing how Sylvia's analysis serves as a foundation for our current interest in whole language. Johnson describes step by step how children learning Key Vocabulary eventually use it to write their own books. Johnson's work with six- and seven-year-olds in poverty in rural Maine is based on

Ashton-Warner's theory, and proves again that Sylvia's work has no cultural or geographical limitation. Johnson writes:

> Helping, or at least allowing, children to bring their own most important images into their school activities is one of the reasons why writing should be done in school, and done even at the youngest ages.
>
> Writing is one very good way for humans to get some distance on problems, to get in touch with what is going on inside ourselves at any age. When a five-year-old's first Words include whom he loves and what he is afraid of, and when a fifth-grader writes in her journal about her anger at her mother, it helps them to deal with their inner selves, just as it helps grown-ups. Writing at any age is cheaper than psychotherapy.[19]

And again:

> Where education in America has made its mistake, I think, is to give too much power to the grid or the structure. Somehow it has gotten turned around. Here is this classification system, they think, for the information of the world, and now we have to be sure that each new member of each new generation has something in each of the spaces on the grid. So we'll put it there, fit it onto his brain the way the metal dividers fit into an ice-cube tray, and fill it. Whether the child has any data for that space or not, whether that has ever been important to him or available to him or not, whether he is ready to grasp that information—that is, attach it to his own structure of the world—or not, we'll just pour information into this grid-mold. Then, since it's easier to do a lot of these pourings at the same time, the classroom becomes the factory, where subjects have to be covered, and children have to be filled with knowledge.
>
> They are, however, already filled with knowledge. What they do learn in school, too often, is that their knowledge, their own work of the last few years, is inadequate, wrong, untrustworthy. It's very easy to get from that state of mind to "I'm inadequate, wrong, somehow untrustworthy." And from there to "tell me what to think," "tell me what to write," "tell me what to read," "tell me what to be," is a dangerously small step.
>
> When we in school allow the children to own their language it is likely that they will come to a sense of ownership and meaning of all their learning, as they had

when they were still toddling through their preschool world[20]

In my 1983 book, *The Sun's Not Broken, A Cloud's Just in the Way: On Child-Centered Teaching*, I show how effectively Key Vocabulary worked to bring parents into the learning process for my four-year-old African-American children in San Francisco's Hunters Point district:

> Teaching children to read helps them gain the respect of their parents. Parents are virtually unanimous in their delight when they hear that I plan to teach their four-year-olds to read. They are moved to smiles and tears of joy when they first hear their children reading words, and are particularly pleased with their children's confidence.
>
> When I teach reading, parents allow me a lot of latitude for a play curriculum because it seems to them that I must know what I'm doing. Reading is the only child's skill that universally impresses adults in our culture. It's what children go to school to learn.[21]

Sylvia's organic reading and writing also shows up in Polly Greenberg's monumental and fascinating book about the beginnings of Head Start in Mississippi in the '60s, *The Devil Has Slippery Shoes: A Biased Biography of the Child Development Group of Mississippi*. Greenberg writes:

> We were trying to separate two giant steps these children are expected to take. One is learning to read, a great step in anyone's life. The other is learning a whole other world, the world of the middle class, which is as far from these children's world as is the world of the Chinese child from the world of a typical middle-class American white child...We don't expect a middle-class child to learn to read in a Chinese classroom and from books written in Chinese. If he is going to learn a foreign language and read in it and understand the culture it is based upon, he usually does it in a later grade. He first learns to read in a familiar milieu and in a 'friendly' language, the one he has always spoken. This is one of Sylvia Ashton-Warner's key themes...[22]

Using the children's own language for beginning reading is the point each of us is making here. If Cynthia produces language other than Standard English, *e.g.* Black English (also called African-American), or English with Spanish word-order or accent, we must respectfully use that. Cynthia won't question our acceptance, since she speaks the code of the people she loves. Adults or other children may tease or "correct" her speech. Interrupting such reactions, I tell them, "That's how Cynthia says that. Different people say things different ways." And I go on using Standard English, as did my mother and father, both children of immigrants, schooled in Standard English by their radios. Thus I provide a model but don't badger the children to follow it. I think we should wait to teach Standard English until Cynthia's spoken language is firmly in place, when she knows that reading is speech written down, when her language belongs to her in all of its aspects and she's able to imagine job interviews and other encounters with the mainstream. This might be in place by fifth grade, if you want a rule of thumb, but then be sure to ask each Cynthia if this is a good time for her to learn to talk the way they do on television—when she is ready, it will be time enough to help her learn Standard English. This way, she will put the new language into a rich context, and will soon own both.

Where they are refused permission to base their teaching of beginning reading upon Key Vocabulary, some teachers use it in addition to the "regulation" method. I think that's worth doing, because teacher and child get to know each other in their meetings, and the child gets at least some words that have importance to him or her. As teachers begin to work with children's own imagery, they grow increasingly confident of their ability to enhance children's accomplishments and self-esteem. In many classrooms teachers "sneak in" a little humanity, looking to Sylvia, among others, for simple ways to show their respect for children at work, despite the impersonal curriculum they are expected to use.

Some teachers reserve Key Vocabulary for children who have failed on the regular path. While it should not be viewed as a remedial method—why fail at all?—I think finding Key Words is far better than once more pushing inconsistent English phonics or sterile look-say at a child. Problems of self-esteem may be hard to surmount with a child who has failed at reading, but writing down words from a person's heart can begin a healing process.

Sylvia's writing influenced the work Vivian Paley describes in *Wally's Stories, Bad Guys Don't Have Birthdays, The Boy Who Would Be a Helicopter* and *You Can't Say You Can't Play*. As she teaches at the University of Chicago Laboratory Schools, Paley assists the children in the process of recording and staging their own stories so they can come to understand and sometimes heal themselves. She takes dictation from children early in the day and later the children perform these dictated stories as plays—*storyplaying*—with the author as director and the adult as facilitator and narrator, extending the Key Vocabulary into time and space. *Storyplaying* is another report from the world of children's inner pictures. The teacher who uses *storyplaying* will naturally encounter key words. Reading instruction can thus continue to evolve organically from this relationship between teacher and child.

[Organic writing] proves to be a startling point of departure into talk that would not occur otherwise. It leads into revelations that range from the entertaining to the outrageous. But, beyond a normal show of interest, you don't comment. You neither praise nor blame; you observe. You let everything come out, uncensored; otherwise, why do it at all?[23]

Late in her life, after Keith died, Sylvia lived with her daughter Jasmine, pregnant, newly widowed, with five children. In *Whenua* (The Land), the house Keith and Sylvia built to retire to, the two widows grieved their losses and raised the children, who also were grieving. Jasmine earned her living weaving baskets, and, during this period, organized the first single parents' group in their city. Grandmother Sylvia worried about Martin, displaced by his mother Jasmine's new baby and grieving over his father David's death. Somehow Martin *needed* to represent the ideas that were tormenting him in his grief:

It was the old baby, Martin, who'd been the toddler round David's feet, who'd shadowed him, hung round his neck, spent his waking hours in the garage studio amid the cane with his father and who'd accompanied him to the railway yards to freight the completed baskets. Now, when not demanding his mother's attention, he'd developed a lethal passion for electric points [outlets] and plugs and connections: 'We're going to lose that boy one of these days, Mummie.' He took to lighting secret matches, he'd light fires in his bedroom early morning before the rest of us woke up and, 'You boys, you must hide that axe. Put it on top of the garden shed.' That he was marvelously handsome with his father's face alleviated nothing. One morning when he accompanied me to the woodheap he stopped and patted the ground, 'Daddy's down there. Unner the ground.'
Wait.
'He's in a box.'
'Yes.'
'He can't walk.'
'No.'
At the door of Selah, 'I've got to go and write now, Mart,' and he cried. 'I can write, Grandma.'
On my left side at the table and a big white card. 'Well what are you going to write?'
'Daddy.'

So in my old way of the pre-fab I take the little chap's key vocabulary each morning and when I didn't he'd cry at my door.

Over some weeks each school morning when the others have gone to school he comes to my door for what he calls his writing and the words surface, the captions of the imagery within: words like *box, ground, plug, points, Mummie, Daniel, goods shed, car, railway, matches* and *axe,* but he's not always sure of them the next morning, from which I suppose there is some other image blocking the channel, jamming the mechanism. The words he doesn't recognise I withdraw so that instead of his vocabulary accumulating it remains but a few. To Jas at her cane, 'I don't know what the image is holding things up. I never do.'

In the sun on the patio with Jas weaving, Martin writing and Daniel asleep, I give Mart stiff white cards to write on and my own big black crayon and he makes these jagged strokes all ways, like mod pop art of the sounds of the new music; abstract. No curves yet. I hold up his own card to him, 'What's that word, Marto?'

'That's Daddy. Now /do it, /do it,' and snatches the card, and holds it up to me. 'What's this word, Grandma?'

'Daddy.'

One morning he comes in from the garage and tells us, 'Daddy's out there. He can walk.'

And Jasmine says, 'Yes.'

'That's the eidetic image, Jas. He's actually seen David. It occurs with some children and with adult artists. I've seen Keith come to my window in Selah, from the vegetable garden, and in his old clothes. Smiling.'

Excitedly, 'I've seen David come in the door. That door, there.'

...[Martin's] recognition of his words remained inaccurate and his behaviour saddening. Jas got the man out to fit covers over the electric points, but Martin made short work of those. And she hid every match in the house and the boys kept the axe out of reach on top of the garden shed until the day he managed to climb up there. Some day, I hoped, the damaging rogue image would surface. So much crying from the little chap.

On the patio one morning with the witnessing trees spreading a roof above us, and with Martin doing his writing, his mother stepped back from the pitcher basket to judge its symmetry. 'Is that right, Mummie, do you think? Doesn't the left shoulder bulge a bit?'

I don't answer at once. 'That boy should have a vocabulary of about thirty by now, the other children did, but there's only a few. I still think there's an image there seizing up the whole show. Like that basket, it has a bulge on one side, so it can't slide through the exit. But look, Jas, at his writing this morning; there are curves coming among those strokes.'

She says, 'What's that writing, Martin?'

'That's the ammulance taking Daddy away.'

So *that* was it and he'd written it himself.

Next morning I hold up to him his own writing from the patio, jagged erratic marks and curves, 'What's this word you wrote, Marto?'

'Ammulance.'

And from then on he recognised the rest. A very beautiful-looking boy, Mart. A rest to see fewer tears on his face.[24]

NOTES TO CHAPTER FOUR

1. This chapter appeared in a somewhat different form in the Claremont Reading Conference 54th Yearbook, 1990.

2. *Thought and Language*, ed. G. Vakar. Trans. E. Hanfmann. Cambridge, MA: MIT Press, 1962, page 75. Sylvia was, unknowingly, a Vygotskian, working where the children's experience was extended by her own into the next stage.

3. From government statistics, reported by Barrington and Beaglehole (see Bibliography): Only about 9% of Maori pupils moved into the upper standards as against about 22% of the Pakeha.

4. *I Passed This Way*, page 262.

5. Quoted by Grace Rotzel in *The School in Rose Valley*, Ballantine, 1971.

6. Unpublished letter, 6 September 1970, to Margaret Albouy, immediately prior to Sylvia's arrival at the Aspen (Colorado) Community School, where Sylvia would teach for just over a year.

7. *Teacher*, page 35.

8. Use of the terms "organic" food and "organic" gardening came much later than this 1940s naming by Sylvia.

9. *Teacher*, page 34.

10. Paul Goodman, *Compulsory Mis-education*, Vintage, 1964, page 26.

11. See my book, *The Sun's Not Broken, A Cloud's Just in the Way: On Child-Centered Teaching*.

12. Dr. Fieldhouse's comments were graciously forwarded to me by Dr. Helen May of Hamilton Teachers College.

13. Bailey is quoted in *Sylvia!*, page 143.

14. *Teacher*, page 32.

15. By cultural difference I mean any of the following: age, gender, race, religion, economic class, degree of centrality or marginality to dominant culture. There is always at least the age difference between teacher and child. In many cases four, five or all of the indicators are different. It is in such cases where teacher and child need an intimate relationship if they are to understand each other.

16. This difference is all the more striking since, frequently, the experimental teachers were given more children with "behavior problems" because they were known to be good with children.

17. Selma Wassermann, *The Vancouver Project: A Study of the Key Vocabulary Approach to Beginning Reading in an Organic Classroom Context*, Simon Fraser University, 1974, pages 116-118.

18. Brown's essay is most easily found in Ira Shor's book, see Bibliography. This quotation, from pages 225-227, is used with permission of the author.

19. *Doing Words*, page 6.

20. *Doing Words*, page 179.

21. Pages 66-67.

22. Page 160.

23. *Teacher*, page 66.

24. *I Passed This Way*, pages 417-419.

FIVE—FINDING SYLVIA A ROOM OF HER OWN:
THE SELAH

I've got to reconcile the woman and the artist or the conflict between them will blow me asunder, scatter my pieces to the ends of the Pacific.[1]
—written by Sylvia *circa* 1942

...we still think we know a "true woman" when we meet one. In our eyes she is a person who does not exercise judgment about when to help others and when to stop, when to worry about their well-being and when to ask them to reciprocate, when to feel their joys and sorrows and when to remember her own, when to try to meet their needs and when to allow them to do things for themselves. She is one who thinks that every intimate needs comfort, every occasion demands indulgence, every relationship requires self-sacrifice.[2]
—written by Jane Roland Martin, 1992

When compared, the statements above, written fifty years apart, are remarkable for two reasons. First, we see how little things have changed after five decades. A woman of the '90s testifies to the same overwhelming and pervasive engulfment by role that was endured by Sylvia and the other women of her time.

A second reading of the two statements reveals how things *have* changed and demonstrates poignantly and powerfully another aspect of Sylvia's dilemma. Jane Martin makes a distinction that Sylvia was not able to see clearly. She eloquently describes the "true woman" in a way that calls the concept into question and prepares each of us to free ourselves from it.

Sylvia's words, on the other hand, do not question the view of womanhood held by her contemporaries. Instead, she takes the true woman as given, pitted against the artist. The conflict between the two is seen as potentially deadly. We gather from her writing that she had been a poetic child artist, her feelings regularly ignored by a prosaic mother and a conventional school. Urgent, strong feeling would regularly build up in her and she felt there was no one who would take the trouble to listen to her woes. She was being raised to be a Victorian, civilized person, who was forbidden destructive expression. In adulthood, her forays at dawn to her study where she could write and paint served to defuse Sylvia's own "impulse to kill."

In her conception of the world there was no room to be both a woman and an independent creative person. Sylvia described her creativity as a monster, *which she perceived as male*. It seems clear from her writing as late as 1971 that her only way out was to sequester her male, creative activities from her female duties. In a letter written that year she said:

> The way of an artist must be this: to live alone with his secrets. Sometimes he releases them in another form through his media but most remain unspoken. The accumulating pressure of what he knows sometimes makes him act defensively though, in terms of his own life, rationally.
> He has a different character of mind whatever country he is in: ingredients in different proportions and he sees life in different perspective. It appears to him that to do what he must is the only thing to do....
> The life of many an artist ends in failure. Seldom does the sun set for him in glory. That it should set in disgrace is not unknown.[3]

It is a mark of how far we have come that today we casually accept the notion that the artistically creative aspects of both men and women may come from their feminine side. It is equally a mark of the desperate situation Sylvia was in that in many ways she rejected her feminine side. In her early thirties, after her breakdown, she concluded that she must separate these parts.

> The only way I see of extricating myself from [teaching] at this late date is to change my occupation for another that pays sufficiently to replace my teacher's salary, that leaves me at home to be a mother to the children and gives me time to be an artist, and this spells writing....In turn this requires that I learn to write and under the present conditions at that; deep and widespread study, a secluded place to work in and...and the *time*.[4]

"Under the present conditions" meant living in isolated Pipiriki, having—or at least feeling the pressure to have—the duties of a wife with three small children, and teaching young children full time. Perhaps she intuitively understood what Adrienne Rich wrote much later:

> *I am a woman in the prime of life, with certain powers*
> *and those powers severely limited*
> *by authorities whose faces I rarely see.*[5]

Every place she lived, from Pipiriki onward, Sylvia had a study. She named them all *Selah:*

> During the centuries of the golden prophets, well before Christ, when the Hebrews sang psalms all day the priest at times would call a pause to give the psalmists a rest, and the word he used was '*Selah.*' A Hebrew word. In charcoal and lipstick I wrote this word '*Selah*' on my door.[6]

A rest. From what? Sylvia lived much of her life in anguish. Her breakdown had frightened her—she must never repeat it! Never again would she feel she had the option of putting the needs of others before the needs of her Self. Her priorities appeared outrageous in an epoch when girls were raised to serve, women were expected to stand by their men mindlessly, and mothers were expected to be silent about their own needs while they put their children's needs first. Even though Keith was willing and able to be the primary parent, Sylvia's neighbors felt her behavior was an affront to respectability, even decency, and Sylvia herself viewed her differences, however necessary, with guilt. The charcoal on her door seems to represent her industry, her art, while the lipstick seems a symbol of her longings for glamour and color.

She wrote at length of the *Selah* and the search for herself in her diary from Pipiriki, *Myself.* This is the most controversial of Sylvia's teaching books, with adherents who love it mightily for its insights and detractors who discount it as self-indulgent and sentimental. I find it very young: awe-inspiring in its brave self-examination, and weak and embarrassing in its occasional self-pity. At any rate, it says a great deal about what a *Selah* is for.

Myself portrays Keith Henderson as the only one who accepted Sylvia's need to create without judging her negatively. Perhaps he carried Sylvia the way Sylvia's wage-earning Mumma had carried her crippled, dreamy Puppa, except that Keith was a tolerant man with an adequate salary while Mumma was intolerant and always broke. His agreement to let Sylvia have the time to work made it possible for her to turn her insight about what she needed from desperate dream into concrete reality. Sylvia didn't have to wrest her work time away from Keith. Instead she struggled with her internalized sense of her community's expectations.

Her culture knew a woman's place, and it wasn't in the *Selah.* Her neighbors knew what woman's work was. It had more to do with putting a nice joint of mutton timely on her family's table than with running away to paint pictures of her passions. But Sylvia knew she needed to express her creativity. The *Selahs* were always organic, either found, a deserted shack, a room somewhere, or constructed from what was plentiful: sods or a cave.

Although *Selah One* dated back to age 20, before she went to college, it was named much later:

> At the back of Te Kainga were buildings which once had been servants' quarters. I spent days scrubbing out these rooms in order to live in them by myself. I was dying to live somewhere by myself. We children had made thousands of little houses in our time but this was the first real place of my own with timbered walls and iron ceiling, a real window and floor and a door that opened and shut. The family called it Sylvie's study but now I see it for what it was: *Selah One.*
> There was already an old table so I put a chair beside it, a pad and a pencil upon it and said I was going to write a book....and if I failed all the way I'd end up at the Wellington Training College to be a dreary teacher, sufficient reason to make anyone write anything. So I sat there and stared out the window on the range.
> I wrote not one word of any book but in time the conditions of silence evoked an idea which all but felled me: instead of writing a book I wrote a letter to the education department in Wellington applying to be zoned [allowed to attend college out of her district] at the Auckland Training College....I wished to attend the Elam School of Art up there, and I told them I had an elder sister in Auckland. What I avoided telling them was that in this way I might extricate myself from the bloody profesh [teaching] and move into commercial art.[7]

At age 31 or 32, before she found a place to study, Sylvia lacked focus:

> I tried to be an artist...I tried to be a writer...I tried to be everything: a good wife, mother and teacher as well, trying to salvage my life simultaneously, and I must say I knew great joy and a lot of it too...[her ellipsis] simply in having a purpose.[8]

Selah Two was brought into being at Pipiriki fourteen years after *Selah One.*[9] Now 34, she sought her workroom deliberately, following what Dr. Allen had said to her: "You mean you don't want to teach other people but to get away in a corner and do it yourself?"[10]

She found an abandoned Maori *whare* (hut) and fixed it up with help from family and friends. *Selah Two* was empty because it had been the scene of a double suicide of the young lovers, Whistle and Mai Mai.[11] For this reason it was *tapu*—unclean and forbidden to Maori:

> 'Please,' from Pearly, 'a big evil spirit it live in Suicide Cottage.'
> ...'How do you know?'
> 'Please the evil spirit in Suicide Cottage it make Whistle and Mai Mai die there.'
> 'Is that why nobody lives in Suicide Cottage?'
> 'Shess. The big evil spirit it live there, the big evil spirit.'
> 'And you're quite sure it doesn't hop in the Pakeha?'
> 'Please the evil spirit don' hop in the Pakeha, the evil spirit.'

Every time she went there to write, the Selah's story reminded her of human vulnerability. Sylvia saw the literary possibilities of this tragic love story and wrote it into several versions of *Greenstone*. Later Michael Firth, in his film, *Sylvia,* showed how spooky the cottage was at first encounter: a Maori man noticing these Pakehas hanging out there responds by collecting green branches and water to purify the site. Sylvia adorned the *Selah* with her images:

> ...the first thing I do in *Selah* is to begin drawing an Egyptian water-carrier holding her vessel upon her head, and I caption it 'Moon of My Delight.'
> Before I start learning to write, however, I just have to put one more drawing on that wall, high in the remaining space: a great bird with wide-stretched wings and iridescent feathers, the whole of the colours in its eyes, and caption it 'My soul, there is a country/far beyond the stars ...' For, at the risk of being sentimental and fatuous, this bird is my hidden spirit.[12]

Throughout her writing we feel the strain between the woman and the writer. This strain was not Sylvia's alone. A year before Sylvia's breakdown, halfway around the world, Virginia Woolf, a woman whose class and education differed substantially from Sylvia's, wrote about the conflict between a woman's need to create and her need to fulfil the expectations of daily life:

> ...to write a work of genius is almost always a feat of prodigious difficulty. Everything is against the likelihood that it will come from the writer's mind whole and entire.

Generally material circumstances are against it. Dogs will bark; people will interrupt; money must be made; health will break down. Further, accentuating all these difficulties and making them harder to bear is the world's notorious indifference. It does not ask people to write poems and novels and histories; It does not need them....'Mighty poets in their misery dead'—that is the burden of their song. If anything comes through in spite of all this, it is a miracle, and probably no book is born entire and uncrippled as it was conceived. But for women...these difficulties were infinitely more formidable. In the first place, to have a room of her own, let alone a quiet room or a sound-proof room, was out of the question, unless her parents were exceptionally rich or very noble, even up to the beginning of the nineteenth century. Since her pin money, which depended on the good will of her father, was only enough to keep her clothed, she was debarred from such alleviations as came even to Keats or Tennyson or Carlyle, all poor men, from a walking tour, a little journey to France, from the separate lodging which, even if it were miserable enough, sheltered them from the claims and tyrannies of their families. Such material difficulties were formidable; but much worse were the immaterial. The indifference of the world which Keats and Flaubert and other men of genius have found so hard to bear was in her case not indifference but hostility. The world did not say to her as it said to them, Write if you choose; it makes no difference to me. The world said with a guffaw, Write? What's the good of your writing?[13]

After the success of *Spinster* and *Teacher,* Sylvia became an idealized figure for tens of thousands of readers. *Myself* isn't idealized. It is a simplified tale of Sylvia's problems: glamour vs. industry, conformity vs. autonomy, love vs. freedom, the mother-wife vs. the artist. Sylvia knew better than to believe her own sugar-clad image. It violated the basis of her philosophy of health: *Acknowledge the demons and the cure will follow.* After the book was scathingly reviewed by the critics, Sylvia wrote about her reasons in writing *Myself* to her friends, American college teachers Jeannette Veatch and Ardelle Llewellen. This letter demonstrates how conscious she had become of the burden of the "true woman" described by Martin:

...I set out deliberately to cure everybody of the conviction that I was a milky *saint*—from *Spinster* and *Teacher*—and apparently I succeeded too well. It was hard to live up to—that halo. I couldn't. It concerned me.

So I let them have it in MYSELF. I don't mind the book failing—they've failed before. I crash every second book. If my public doesn't like the heroine (*Bell Call*) that is just the rough and tumble of writing.

You mourn the loss in dollars but I live cheerfully enough and carry on. But in MYSELF my reader doesn't like *me*. Now that hurts. I didn't anticipate that they would stop liking *me*. All I thought I was doing was removing the heavy halo. I've been sad...So here you find a writer *typed*. Unless I write romantically about spinsters and children, I'm unacceptable whereas really, I've done that subject to the very bottom of it. But I can't help that. I'm a person, adult, and am interested in other things as well...The artist in me is glad to be free of the weighty halo. The woman in me is sad but the artist in me is happy.[14]

I'm not sure we should believe every word of this report, but it gives another perspective to her story. Sylvia had something to say but couldn't say it the way she felt it, for fear it would be found *feminine,* the critics' curse on a woman's writing.

To write she needed silence:

Twenty minutes to walk up bringing water from the creek, ten minutes to set the fire, sweep room, wash hands, change into slippers and then get out my books. Absolutely thrilling.[15]

I believe that rather than harm me the routine will spruce me up, and from my study as I go along toward my obscure goal—to be a worthwhile person—I learn things that confirm it, and from experience, too. Do the word study at home in the early morning but leave essays and drafting for *Selah;* in fact leave anything creative at all for the silence of *Selah.*[16]

In other moods, Sylvia dreamed of other uses for her special space:

Selah is the house I've built before in the brilliance of wishful fantasy, emerging into reality...Here could be the fresh air of independence, the miracle of solitude, the pocket of flowers that I saw, of music, study and painting...the bedroom done in chintz with pretty curtains blowing the dead away, the kitchen equipped as a study and the big front room as a place of music with floor rugs, wine and piano. Elegant people will come with their hair quietly parted. Terrific conversations plunging through till morning, all sorts of heart-to-heart revelations ...romantic, electric, exclusive. Looking newly at Suicide Cottage I reeled with inspiration.[17]

Fantasies aside, Sylvia used her *Selahs* for her original purpose, to paint, to write, to be with her thoughts. She could answer her critics, as she does in this essay which seems never to have been published:

LOVE[18]

I've just this minute read a letter from a man who attended the Refresher Course for teachers of Maori children at Ardmore. It said they all felt up there that I "stressed too much the FEAR aspect within the child when other more positive 'inner urges' would have served better as a basis for building your Key Vocabulary."

How I like to claim that I am easily corrected and am able to change my mind! But this would mean that I would have to first deny that fear is the most powerful of the instincts. Whereas to be technical, it is no less than self-preservation.

Look at our world today. What do you think of the power of fear in it. How are we going to achieve peace in a world until we have dealt with fear. How are we going to achieve peace in a mind until we have dealt with the worry. And was anything alive ever born without the sense of fear; without the instinct of self-preservation. After all if you are going to do anything at all, anything between teaching a class and splitting an atom, you've first got to be alive to do it. How could I "stress fear too much." Fear doesn't need any help.

If only we held something...some ace...that was stronger than fear. But ...psychologically speaking, there's nothing. Yet, reading the biographies of great souls, (if I might be indulged in the use of so indeterminate, so disputed, a word as "soul") it is not unusual to come upon some further power that proves itself stronger. Even in a mean soul, for that matter. Time and again we come upon a second strange force that silences fear in crises: even without a crisis sometimes. Look in our own lives. Look back into history. Go back as far as you like. Go back as far as Paul: something or other...what was it now..."casteth out fear."

The *Selahs* gave the woman-as-artist some turf where she could house her masculine monster:

> Keith and I and the school were in full bloom to the point where my private work actually fused with teaching, believe it or not. My capacity to get over and forget recurring disasters and betrayals rated as another craft again. I could even conceive the idea of a future as a teacher side by side with Keith provided the department let me progress and not keep me treading *water*, and if the artist in me would sign the deal.
>
> But that artist was no romantic wraith feeding on dreams any more; he was a monster from outer space inhabiting the mind, a ruthless invader, demanding, fierce, bumping round knocking things over, jealous of the school and not prepared to accommodate either the wife or the teacher. The monster was the other man in the home whom I knew Keith resented, however consistently he helped to supply the conditions for my work, from support at school to fires in *Selah* and to giving me time. A man could be expected to be able to contain a physical rival whom he could see and fight and rout, which in fact had already occurred at Fernhill over a man in a pulpit,[19] but what chance had any human husband of shaping up to a lover intangible, invisible, yet voracious and permanent? If Keith also feared him he had good reason. Very seldom would Keith mention my work or praise me for it but I knew why and I'd learnt not to bring up the subject. In the interest of domestic harmony I'd keep the monster out of the home, lock him up in some *Selah* apart from the house, a Maori whare, a cave, a sod hut or in the shed in this back yard where I could go to him like a secret paramour and let him have his way with me, then return home again as a wife. Two distinct lives.[20]

Every time I read this passage I assumed it was hyperbole, Sylvia going on dramatically about the separation of her artistic and her family lives. But when I met Sylvia's daughter, Jasmine, in 1988, and asked about a book I thought Sylvia would have kept in her *Selah*, Jasmine told me, "I'm afraid I can't help you with that sort of problem, because I don't know about such things. My mother kept her intellectual life separate."

There was a period of some months when it seemed that Keith would have to go and fight in World War II. At this time, trips to the *Selah* often carried a burden of guilt:

> ...I came to *Selah* for a few hours of solid work but I cannot settle...K, although he doesn't say so, wants me to talk to while he works outside. I'll remember this day when he's gone, I thought. This will come back and haunt me. So intensely do I feel the need of me at home that for the first time I want to leave *Selah*.[21]

Mothers know this particular vice: wanting time for oneself and always knowing there are family chores that must be done. Mothers with outside jobs know it still better.

In another context:

> S: "There's no need for you to take on my afternoon work."
>
> K: "But my work loses its value unless you are happy. Everything loses its value. Your contentment comes before my work."
>
> S: "I'm happy."
>
> K: "No you're not."
>
> He looked at me with interest. I went on, "You're not getting as much time for study as I am. You're the real mother of this family; I'm just one of the children. We must share the time."
>
> He pushed the kettle over the flames. "But your study means more to you than mine does to me."
>
> S: "I question it. But in any case that's not my point. Your work means more to me than my own does to me because your work involves your contentment and that comes before my work with me."
>
> He was interested but looked doubtful.
>
> "It's the truth," I added. "Unless you are happy in your work mine is valueless to me."
>
> K examined my face as though he was seeing it for the first time.
>
> "It may not be apparent," I said, "but I love you and you come first in the world with me, before everything, before anybody. You and the children. My family and home are more to me than my work. If it came to the choice it would be my work that went overboard. No doubt I've appeared to be a failure in the home but that is not indicative. Do you feel I've failed you in the home?"

I called on all my courage to ask this question which could draw a devastating answer.

He put out two cups and saucers. "Well, it has crossed my mind that you shouldn't have married."

Catastrophe! "But I've been a good mother! Look at me all through my babies. How I stuck to them on the Coast."

K: "Yes. But what I mean is that a person, any person, with your inclinations should not marry. You should have gone on with your work. Marriage has sidetracked you."

S: Desperately on the defensive, "I wash and dress the little boys in the morning, and Jonquil.[22] I feed them."

K: "I know. What I mean is that people like you with talents and ideas should be undisturbed by marriage."

S: "Ah but you see! I wouldn't have had these desires at all if I hadn't married. When I didn't teach and had no babies I hardly lifted a brush. Hardly did a thing. The *need* to study, to do, to make, to think, *arises* from being married. I need to be married to work."

He poured the boiling water on the tea. "I still think that you should be allowed your work in preference to my being allowed mine. Your desire is stronger than mine"...Neither of us lowered the flag, neither won, and we haven't talked about that since, but the part about his coming before my work must have registered and held for there's been a tenderness in his manner toward me like the reappearance of the sun, and that close feeling has returned.[23]

To this day most people in America and New Zealand assume that giving first priority to one's job is the prerogative of a father but not of a mother. Sylvia was so crowded by the implications of this assumption that she named her first novel, about a working, productive teacher, *Spinster.*

Sylvia's creative 'monster' demanded discipline in his work—but Sylvia, the mother, had little or no discipline in relation to traditional female chores. Sylvia was often upset about her inadequacy as wife and mother, but this contradictory pull was one cost she paid for being unconventional. Did it bother her that Keith was the one preparing and serving the tea while they had this discussion? She couldn't rise above her culture's assumptions about gender roles, although he, apparently, could.

In 1980, too late to do Sylvia's reputation any good, Letty Cottin Pogrebin wrote, validating her choices:

> Let Father get the dinner while Mother and the boys play. Those idyllic images of the woman approvingly watching her 'men' cavorting beyond the kitchen window as she scrubs the grass stains out of yesterday's play-clothes or warms the soup for their lunch are propaganda for woman-as-spectator. Your daughter is more likely to want to be a woman if it doesn't mean giving up the action for a view from the kitchen window.[24]

Sylvia was among those brave souls who, having suffered mental illness and recovered, resolve to live differently, never to return to a state where she finds her life to be of small value. This brings about a willingness to do uncharacteristic things: go into debt, isolate oneself, exercise, run away, behave irresponsibly, end an addiction, anything rather than re-enter the abyss. Sylvia, by her example, encourages readers to honor their own needs. Her children were cared for by their father and this was enough to permit her to disregard the general opinion that only a mother could raise children. She considered the *Selahs* and the work she did in them as essential for avoiding additional breakdowns.

Myself is full of the hum, buzz and mutter of small town gossip. The neighbors, characteristically unaware of the need to create, have their own ideas about what *Selah Two* is for:

> 'Everyone says you come up here to meet Tom Snowdon.'
> 'Do they really?'[25]

Ominously, rumor reached Sylvia that the owner was going to take back the cottage. Sylvia wanted other people to shun the place:

> 'This place is haunted,' [blind Kata's mother] said. 'I wouldn't live here for quids.'
> I didn't intend anyone to want to live here for quids. 'You're dead right,' I said, 'it is. I wouldn't sleep here at night.'[26]

Sylvia lost *Selah Two* suddenly, when the landowner indeed reclaimed it to process his sheep in. *Selah Three* was very different, a cave cut into the riverbank. Sylvia carved a Buddha over the fireplace in this *Selah*, and wrote at this period about taking pleasure in art that was impermanent.

In March, 1945, as they arrived at their new post at Waiomatatini, thirty-seven-year-old Sylvia ignored their residence and scanned the scene to determine where her fourth *Selah* would be:

...the first thing my roving eye sought was some kind of *Selah*...Nothing. No Maori *whares* [huts], haunted or otherwise, no roadman's hut, no army hut, no shed, not even a clump of trees ...without four walls and a roof to call my own, without my regular ration of silence, without my minimum thinking conditions, I could never be a productive person.

In the brilliance of vision that crisis brings I saw what I would do. While the children ran excitedly ahead through the gate and K looked across at the school I saw in mind a small place I would build myself of sods from the ground, enclosed in new-grown trees. I looked down on the ground and dug in a high heel of suede to examine the turf,...It clicked on the contour of stones.[27]

They made the dream into reality:

An iron roof he puts on it, a little stove in it, a marvelous tube chimney and the sweetest door with leather hinges but it takes a long time. On this unpainted timber door I printed the key words, *Selah Four;* for me to study, learn to write, paint, dance and consult my instincts in, for unless I created for myself under my own power an alternative source of income to teaching, unless I exercised my homespun function of an artist, I'd decompose from the spirit outward.[28]

Spinster's protagonist, Anna, has a *Selah,* too. Anna mentions this *Selah,* based on the suicide cottage at Pipiriki, many times. Anna faces her internal conflicts there:

I do no more...than pick up my 6B pencil with the softest black lead and draw a small girl crying. True, there are no such things in the new Imported Books, with which the Maori infant rooms have been supplied, no such things as tears, and nothing so unrespectable as emotion. Neither is there dancing nor punches in the [stomach], nor screams of laughter and embraces. Butthere are these things in my books. I make this little girl. I draw her in pencil first, a few lines-worth of long dress, bare feet, straggly hair and tears. I choose the finest of my pre-war brushes to turn the paint the colour I mean and, by the time the rain has settled down heavily on the low roof, here is this little girl wailing from the page.

> I'm portraying child drama in these early books. Open-eyed I'm going into another sure mistake. Another avoidable mistake.[29]

On occasion, Anna allows co-worker Paul Vercoe to invade her space and, instead of attending to her work, she visits with him. But the *Selah* is a place of honesty and discipline, and she realizes her error:

> Art and work should not be put aside, since from them comes vision. I should have put Paul aside for my brushes and reading and then what little was left of my time for him would have been of more value ....I was unfaithful to my work. I gave him quantity.
> But not quality.[30]

The *Selahs* let Sylvia breathe. Her creative work, done at dawn, supported her teaching, refreshed her and gave form to the material she gathered during school hours. Breathing out and then breathing in gave a shape to her days and became another metaphor in her teaching. [There is more about this in Chapter 9.]

In her late fifties Sylvia the author and Keith the headmaster built a house with her *Selah* at one end of the gracious home overlooking the Bay of Plenty. It was the end of genteel poverty, and anticipated Keith's retirement:

> After parsonages and residences all [Keith's] life and school residences the whole of my life we built our large home, *Whenua* [pronounced fain' oo uh, the Maori word meaning the land], on the harbour front: a long stone house on a long high bank overlooking the long blue sea, designed for full-scale gatherings and to house overseas guests, mine as well as his, with a music room half the size of a hall opening out upon a deck to the water.[31]

After Keith's death and during her travels abroad Sylvia had the *Selah* rebuilt:

> In my absence [in Vancouver] I had the architect expand it to a self-contained apartment—one large room all windows, kitchen in corner part of it—a large bathroom. Three doors opening on three patios. Trees, all four years bigger. The walls, all black, off white, painted and nothing whatever on them, just the changing

changing lights and shadows. The ceiling high peaked, dark panelled. No furniture. Only four essentials: a table, chair, a bed in a corner, stereo, and mid-centre, another grand piano. Through the windows over the garden between the trees, the soft summer sea. The life irreducible.[32]

Back home after her three years in North America, approaching seventy, finishing her autobiography and planning to stop writing, she came to *live* in *Selah*.

I get on with my work in *Selah* where I also sleep. No [guest] needs help from me; all you do is supply the conditions for the mind to take care of itself, and the body too half the time, while the traveller unwinds his tight knots to see ahead more clearly, for *Whenua* has this secret healing quality which has nothing to do with me.[33]

Sylvia won a victory over the self-sacrifice and suffocation that was the lot of working women of her time. She also tells us something about what this victory cost her, from the neurotic battles with herself in *Myself* through the drinking she lets us glimpse in *Spinster* to the longing for complete freedom in *Bell Call* and the devastating fantasies of the femme fatale in *Incense to Idols*.[34]

Perhaps the most poignant cost of having an unconventional spirit was feeling rejected by her New Zealand compatriots, which Sylvia bemoaned in *I Passed This Way*.[35] Lonely, but with respect for her own judgment and her need to leave treasure behind her, Sylvia wrote for publication until the last few years of her life, and in her autobiography looked back from age seventy with satisfaction on what she had accomplished.

The *Selahs* represented Sylvia's attention to herself: maybe a cave was all she had to work in, but by God she had a cave of her own. Eventually she had the *Selah* at *Whenua*, elegantly functional and gracious, fulfilling the dream of the poor rural child, proof of her triumphant survival and her abundant life.

Sylvia won the struggle she showed us in *Myself*. She became what later feminists would call "a passionate knower" with "a way of weaving [her] passions and intellectual life into some recognizable whole."[36] Sylvia shows her readers how to take for ourselves the room we need to live vividly, tunefully and in the present.

NOTES TO CHAPTER FIVE

1. These words can be found in *Myself*, page 115. This book, published in 1967, is a recasting of Sylvia's diary written from the late 1930s through World War II.

2. *The Schoolhome: Rethinking Schools for Changing Families*, page 110.

3. From unpublished letter to Bruce Thomas, administrator of Aspen Community School, May 8, 1971.

4. *I Passed This Way*, page 294, her ellipsis and emphasis.

5. "I Dream I'm the Death of Orpheus" in *Poems, Selected and New, 1950-1974*. NY, WW Norton, 1975.

6. *Myself*, page 77.

7. *I Passed This Way*, page 182.

8. *I Passed This Way*, pages 287-8.

9. *I Passed This Way*, page 297.

10. *I Passed This Way*, page 282.

11. *I Passed This Way*, page 302.

12. *I Passed This Way*, pages 297-8.

13. In *A Room of One's Own*, Harcourt, Brace and World, 1929, pages 53-4. Printed here with permission.

14. Unpublished letter, October, 1967.

15. *Myself*, page 80.

16. *Myself*, page 81.

17. *Myself*, pages 116-7.

18. A document in the Sylvia Ashton-Warner archive at Boston University Special Collections.

19. Sylvia had had a flirtation with a Reverend Tom Carr. This apparently worried Keith but came to nothing. She fictionalized this romance in *Incense to Idols*.

20. *I Passed This Way*, pages 360-1.

21. *Myself*, page 108.

22. *Myself* is a fictionalized account of a passage in Sylvia's life. Jonquil is a fictionalized version of Sylvia's daughter, Jasmine.

23. *Myself*, pages 92-3.

24. *Growing Up Free, Raising Your Child in the Eighties*, page 357.

25. *Myself*, page 105.

26. *Myself*, page 144.

27. *Myself*, pages 232–3.

28. *I Passed This Way*, page 320.

29. *Spinster*, page 39.

30. *Spinster*, pages 146-7.

31. *I Passed This Way*, page 369.

32. Letter to Jeannette Veatch, undated but around September 1973.

33. *I Passed This Way*, page 92.

34. The reader interested in women's choices is urged to read *Composing A Life* by Mary Catherine Bateson.

35. Her children had differing reactions to their mother's peculiarity, remembering her with complex emotions and their father, more simply, with love.

36. Belenky, et al. *Women's Ways of Knowing*, page 141.

SIX —TELLING CREDIBLE & INCREDIBLE STORIES: DO WE SEEK FACTS OR TRUTH?

Touch the true voice of feeling and it will create its own vocabulary and style.

—Mary Coleridge

... the crucial distinction for me is not the difference between fact and fiction, but the distinction between fact and truth. Because facts can exist without human intelligence, but truth cannot.

—Toni Morrison[1]

Today urban educators are learning what indigenous people have never forgotten: that people learn best and most from stories. Patricia Grace, in her remarkable novel, *Potiki,* tells of a Maori child who is frightened by school: "He says they've got no stories for him."[2] Of course, this school had stories to teach this child, but they were irrelevant to his culture.

Sylvia's greatest successes came from her books, as her father's successes came from telling stories. She came to believe that story is the most human medium, and the finest teacher.

Legions of admirers appreciate Sylvia's wonderful knack for making stories. Fact or fiction, her stories communicated to her pupils, and pleased and instructed millions of readers around the world. Her stories provide us with mirrors that can show us our past, our present and our potentiality. Moreover, they also show us how we can evoke new stories from others.

Sylvia's eleven books were published between 1959 and 1978. Fiction and nonfiction alike, ten of those books are substantially autobiographical.[3] Clearly, her autobiographies weren't strictly objective nor was her fiction strictly fictional.

In all her writing we can see the novelist and teacher's interest in a good and useful story, rather than an historian's interest in facts. This chapter looks at three of the novels to see what stories Sylvia had to tell, then at accusations—which arise, mainly in New Zealand—that she was a storyteller in another sense, that of being a liar.

In Sylvia's best novels, *Spinster, Incense to Idols* and *Greenstone,* she used the flying carpets, seven-league boots and sea serpents[4] from the magical side of her mind. These novels employ embroidery and artifice, but aren't wholly fictional: Looking in her autobiographies we can find the history behind many of the fictional scenes.

Spinster[5] retold—as a novel, so she could get it published—Sylvia's work teaching initial reading. About thirty percent of *Teacher*—a nonfiction account of the same work—and *Spinster* overlap in content, some of it word for word. The reader believes in the impetuous, passionate, earnest, fragile and murderous children of *Spinster* and trusts that they are generated from the children Sylvia actually taught.

Spinster quickly earned Sylvia world recognition. To this day her audience understands Anna's ambivalence toward her work and her life, fears the Inspectors with her, and grieves with her for her losses. The discovery of the Key Vocabulary is spun out, delicately, the way it must have happened. The heroine balks at the foolishness of teaching rural children about watering cans, wants to *connect the insides of children to their outsides* and is frequently troubled because she is intruding on her pupils. Like her author, Anna reads Herbert Read and works in her *Selah*. The novel gives us unrequited love, sudden death and hope. The children need not only their teacher, but also the reader, cheering them on. Readers did, and they do, and they will.

Sylvia's second novel, *Incense to Idols*, is very different. It's about a destructive, creative pianist who had a hard, motherless childhood, a woman who is an emotional volcano. Because Sylvia is describing her inner imagery here, I think this novel tells us a great deal about her psychological struggles.

The heroine, Germaine de Beauvais, is recently widowed with enough money to do what she likes. She has come to New Zealand from her native France to study with a maestro who left France in the midst of a scandal. Sylvia's editor, Robert Gottlieb, wrote to Sylvia, saying that, in his "stereotypical view," French mistresses were small, mean and shop-keeper-minded. Sylvia replied that she thinks of Germaine not as a mistress but as a courtesan, "and some of them had largeness."[6]

Germaine is a glamorous, amoral concert pianist who dresses in a vast wardrobe of elegant clothing and, for reasons of privacy and intrigue, lives in New Zealand as "Mrs. Jones." Though—or possibly because—it is lurid, *Incense* received good reviews when it came out in 1960, especially in *Time,* whose unsigned review compared Germaine to Molly Bloom! James K. Baxter called the book "strange, makeshift, crude, showy, sophisticated, [and] magnificent."[7]

The inflection of the book is unique: a running inner-voice monologue. Baxter again:

> We see Germaine's world solely through her own eyes. The profound validity of the novel lies in its subjective truth. The creative monologue is Sylvia Ashton-Warner's natural medium, as it is Henry Miller's

or Samuel Beckett's and while she could perhaps polish it more, she would be a fool to abandon it.[8]

When Germaine's mother died giving birth to her:

> They gave me to my father a minute old. He was at the piano playing. He put me on top of the pianoforte and went on playing. And that's where I stayed all my babyhood waking and sleeping. I lived on that grand; I heard every note. The sound of the music has not left me till this day. I hear music all the time; everything from chansons through hymns to jukeboxes. I can hear it this very minute; I hear a chanson "May the night bear my breath away." I can relieve myself only by playing. I'm not a real musician; I don't really love music. It's music that loves me.[9]

While Germaine was performing as soloist in a piano concerto under the baton of her husband, he collapsed and died. She reports that she missed two and one-half bars of the music. We are to understand her as a woman of little sentiment and great drive.

Pitted against this fascinating and powerful woman, sometimes disapproving of her but inevitably succumbing to her sensuous invitation, are five men. The mightiest of these is an obsessive, judgmental Christian minister whose Jehovah makes him no happier than Germaine's idol, Baal, makes her. The minister takes his text from Hosea, serving up terrible retribution to those who forget God, and from Jeremiah, condemning those who burn incense to idols. Germaine, sounding a bit like Sylvia Ashton-Warner, truculently maintains that she has neither forgotten nor misidentified God, that she simply needs the evidence of her senses to believe in anything.

The other men, a student, a doctor, a drunkard and the maestro, are all tragically flawed, but give Sylvia many opportunities to describe the tension between the artist's perspective and the rest of the world's. Sylvia editorializes about war, God, atheism, art, sex, motherhood and beauty. She reminds herself, her characters and her readers that Christ was a passionate man.

In the course of *Incense to Idols,* Germaine, a literal *femme fatale,* devastates each of the men in a different way, losing herself in the awful bargain. Why Sylvia wrote this book—her second published—was not evident to me at first, since it clearly doesn't fit with her other work. But her description of two dreams she held, side by side, during her early twenties makes it clearer:

> ... I'd dream ... there was the studio with paint and a piano, the teapot and cup and saucer, the frying pan and sausages, one bed and only me there. It was a

that increasingly featured austerity and asceticism and there was no man in it.

Yet, prospering side by side with this, was another the very opposite, a new one I hadn't worn before in which I've finally slimmed down, become arrestingly beautiful and wear exotic clothes, I'd meet the man of all men, tall as usual, dark, handsome and rich, who'd fall madly in love with me...and be married in yards of white satin and a veil.

Strangely, that was as far as the action went; the wedding was all. I didn't seek any afterwards. Both dreams were doing well though entirely unrelated to each other. The wedding dream flared when I was at the hostel talking love-affairs with the girls but when I was marooned at school I favoured the recluse one.[10]

Her heroine's punishing disasters and suicide at the book's end may represent the judgments of others which Sylvia had felt and internalized. She may have always grieved that she couldn't, at least in some respects, have Germaine's freedoms and adventures.

In *Incense* we wallow in the conflict between sex and fear. Sylvia writes about men as Germaine's sex objects in a way that would have been less surprising if this book had come after, say, Erica Jong's 1973 book *Fear of Flying.* In 1960, in New Zealand, *Incense* was so sexually free that, although Sylvia had not yet traveled outside New Zealand, she imported Germaine from France.

But Germaine seems to me far more superficial than Sylvia would have been *had* she chosen an artist's life. Just as Sylvia became analytic about her teaching, I think she'd have been analytic about an artist's life too: Such self-analysis was part of her temperament. *Incense*, while it permitted her to discharge some tumultuous neurotic longings, trivializes and vulgarizes such a life. It was, after all, a life she didn't know. So she went back to writing what she knew.

Greenstone, Sylvia's novel of her family of origin, published in 1966, depicts Puppa as bright-eyed, curly-haired, crippled and a wonderful storyteller. On the other hand, Mumma is the breadwinner and woodchopper who, despite her violence and coldness toward them, wants her children to be accomplished. Mumma causes Puppa to lose an eye. In reality this didn't happen, but rather than building on historical logic, this novel has a psycho–logical or mytho–logical basis: Mumma seemed so violent that she could have blinded Puppa. Other events, intimate and far-reaching, are both invented and remembered. Puppa makes wonderful stories about the many children, the white ones and Huia, the Maori princess whose father and grandfather were white. The stories include *Greenstone,* a magnificent allegory about the struggle between the whites and the Maori for the land of New Zealand/Aotearoa. Here is a part of it:

"I was dying," replied Rikirangi, "but I wanted so much to see how the sun rose that I decided not to die. No sun rises in the land of spirits."

"You have risen by yourself," cried the [white man]. "That is no less wonderful than the rising of the sun."

"There is little other thought in my mind than of rising; rising again and again."

... "A boy of your caliber," [the white man] remarked, "is certainly worth knowing. I have learned much from you. I shall be proud to protect you."

"Will you," asked Rikirangi, "return my greenstone? It will bring a curse upon you."

"I will not return your greenstone."[11]

This story-within-a-story is more wonderful because it is surrounded by what Sylvia's teacher's ear has mastered: before the story we hear the authentic cacophony of getting the children settled in. ...

"Now I once heard of a Maori boy who..."

"No, a princess," from the white ones, "with hair like a cloud at sunset."

"No, no," from Lance, "we've worked out that princess business. Get on with this story about this boy. I'll put up with him being a Maori."

".... a little Maori boy called...."

"Not little," from Lance. "Make him my age."[12]

... and after the official end of the story, the sound of their need to make sense of what they've just heard:

Richmond wakes beneath the bed and Trelawny, holding the old baby, accuses, "The white man didn't give Rikirangi back his greenstone."

Huia, "That was the land."[13]

How did such stories come about? In 1977 Sylvia was interviewed on *TV New Zealand*[14] by Jack Shallcrass, a New Zealand educator who had become her friend when both opposed the Vietnam War. Sylvia spoke in warm tones about her childhood, "when all the [creative] channels were open." As one watches her remembering, probably accurately, the creative possibilities of that period, she seems also in complete denial of the pain of her early childhood, when her schoolteacher mother left her in the care of her crippled, chair-bound father, who couldn't go to her when she was in need but could only respond when she came to him. According to her writing, as a child she was quite unhappy with the middling, prosaic, ordinary place she occupied in the family. Her talent and her ambition went unrecognized by her parents, siblings and teachers. But in the interview she rewrote dull black-and-white history into blazing technicolor. Sylvia did this all the time.

Both *Spinster* and *Greenstone* are romances about Sylvia's real world. She has taken poetic license and told the stories in enchanted, high colors.

Weaving gorgeous stories from drab reality expressed Sylvia's spirit but left her open to criticism. Sylvia's authorized biographer, Lynley Hood,[15] takes exception to Sylvia's colors, and seems to be more interested in uncovering discrepancies between what Sylvia wrote and historical facts. For instance, Hood writes:

> By the end of the summer Mama, Daphne, Sylvia, Norma, Marmaduke and Evadne were living at the back of a boarding house in what, from Sylvia's description, sounded like a dilapidated shed, "... very small, unlined, unpainted, broken panes, they kept their tools and sacks and things there..." But it wasn't a shed. It was a cottage—kitchen, living room, two bedrooms—built in 1905 for the parents of the owner of Dean Court, the boarding house. People were still living in the cottage in 1985—surely it can't have been that terrible in 1919?[16]

On pages 66-67 of *Sylvia!* Hood postulates that the Hendersons marry earlier than planned because Sylvia has a "phantom pregnancy." Then she concludes:

> But this isn't a novel. So we just have to note that Sylvia is concealing something about her wedding. And we don't know what it is.

Lynley Hood reads Sylvia in a journalist's terms. By contrast, I am trying in this book to examine the texture of Sylvia's life for clues to how we can become better teachers and be more supportive to children. We can be sure Sylvia attempted to say the things she must—to tell her stories—but what was their relationship to facts? Did she report accurately? Should we care?

I think Sylvia rewrote everything. Some of the rewriting made her pain easier to bear. But much of it served her goals in teaching. In the next chapter I will show you a way of making stories which I hope you will try, because I too believe that stories help us learn. They must be based on our strengths and help us overcome fears, and never used to cover up our weaknesses and errors. Stories are teachers' best tools.

Sylvia developed Key Vocabulary,[17] Breathing In and Out,[18] and curriculum which emerges from children's interests, not only in the face of her own emotional undercurrents, but in confrontation, as well, with the time and place in which she lived. This took courage. In a perceptive passage, Hood writes:

... magical transmutation of unbearable reality into bearable fiction was a technique of coping that shaped Sylvia's autobiographical writing throughout her life.[19]

To this day Sylvia is dismissed or derided by many of her countrymen and women who were offended by the way she made up stories. Her refusal to give precedence to doing one's respectable, orthodox duty as wife and mother infuriated her critics and won Sylvia her passionate admirers. She believed in the redemption that comes from a good story, the healing that comes from using one's gifts to convert the mean and drab and daily into the fantastic and glorious. This belief—which saves Tinker Bell in every performance of *Peter Pan*—goes beyond *fact* to *truth*.

Jeanne Marie Bear of the Sylvia Ashton-Warner Society writes:

Those interested in catching Sylvia in "lies" don't recognize the utility of the fantasies and how they led Sylvia to her creative methods of teaching and to her compassion for children, understanding their pain *and* their creativity.

After reading a chapter in Hood's book which, among other things, says:

She compensated by making up stories about her family; to explain her father's lack of visible occupation she claimed to her classmates that he was an artist. Before long her stories of Warner grandeur began to grow out of control, and the reality of her family life at Te Whiti became for Sylvia a "smouldering explosive secret."

Bear writes:

It's tempting to mix psychologizing with pigeonholing and judgmentalism—at a safe distance where you can't be corrected—instead of with understanding and illumination. But psychology was developed (not, I think, with malice) to explain away and destroy what others saw as sacred reality, spiritual crises, and inspired creativity...the only reality in which to understand what Sylvia did with her emotions and mind.[20]

I sometimes comfort myself saying: *I'm a grownup and I can do anything I want to.* This is illogical, inaccurate, untrue. I am in fact limited by courtesy, economic considerations, law and good judgment. As a child I thought grownups were simply free. Yet this true lie still lifts my spirit.

Sylvia wrote about a child in her class and his grandfather:

> Now Matawhero is the grandson of the Chairman
> of the School Committee, of whom, I blush to say, I am
> not wholly unaware as a woman. He is the biggest size I
> have seen in men and Matawhero is the smallest.
> However they meet on one thing. Lying. But I like lying.
> The imaginative stuff, you know. Not the dull foreseeable
> line.[21]

Bill Cliett, recalling 1971, wrote to me confirming that Sylvia's imagination was committed to the making of a good story, and thus to connecting with the kind of truth that transcends facts:

> Sylvia said to me, after dinner one night in Aspen,
> "The only thing I can see in fact is that it is a point of
> departure towards the unreal." I took it as a comment
> on the importance of the imagination, fact being merely
> the springboard or launchpad.[22]

Finding the truth in Sylvia's stories is more useful than checking her facts and then dismissing her and her stories by calling her a liar. For example, in *Greenstone* Sylvia casts herself in two roles, a dense and artful reconstruction of what was once the central conflict of her life. Susanna, the drab Pakeha child with a history like Sylvia's own, and Huia, the lovely, graceful Maori princess, who appreciates enchanting stories and has great plans for her future, represent two sides of Sylvia. The novel brought her historical child-self and her fantasy child-self together—and helped Sylvia approach the integration she sought all her life. I think that Sylvia always imagined herself to be Huia the Princess and often remembered that she was Susanna the Ugly. Sylvia's critics tend to ignore Huia's magical, spontaneous, resolute perspective and instead to attend critically to Susanna's perspective—dismal, earthbound and apprehensive.

The facts we choose to notice are reflections of how we perceive the world, not necessarily the way the world actually is. The "factual" recitation of history is also a story—colored, just as much as other "lying," by what seems to make sense, to have an acceptable consistency, even at the expense of complex meaning. For example, the "historical" paintings of glorious Columbus and his beribboned men descending to meet the humble "Indians" misrepresent the probable reality: that the Native Americans were healthy and well attired while the scurvy-ridden, dirty, exhausted sailors were a sorry sight.

Lying isn't the only charge laid at Sylvia's feet. Hood makes a case that Sylvia focused upon European (and American) material: *The Toy Maker's Dream, Wedding of the Painted Doll, Lochinvar, Hiawatha,* in her teaching of Maori children. I'm sure there was some European material out in the bush on her own where Sylvia was without a single model of Maori-centered teaching. But in 1961 in New York when I read *Teacher*, Ashton-Warner was the author who first conveyed to me a clear picture of how one goes about crossing a cultural gulf. She dramatically and specifically warned of the dangers of colonizing a child's mind.[23]

In 1990, Sylvia's friend Joy Alley told me that in the '40s they both believed, as young women, that anything from Europe was superior to anything from New Zealand. It seems that Maori music and dance were taught by Maori adults, while Sylvia produced these European-based dramas for large audiences. I suggest that these extravaganzas bought her some tolerance from the establishment, thus protecting the Key Vocabulary and the intense arts program. We teachers often have to fight to include in our curricula those things currently deemed "frills." Teaching school in New York City during the '60s, I remember the official intolerance of children reading silently during school time and how I felt at risk permitting it![24]

In *Spinster* and *Teacher* we read about Key Vocabulary, which is to this day an excellent model of cultural fit: When Maori children choose their words, reading is based on Maori culture. Getting the text from the mind of the child prevents a teacher from forcing an alien culture upon that child. Sylvia's Key Vocabulary was extraordinary at a time when schools were called "Native," English was the only language spoken or tolerated in school and the domestic arts—sewing, cleaning, cooking, all in the British tradition—predominated.

Hinewirangi was Sylvia's student at age eight. Today a distinguished international poet and an activist around the world for indigenous peoples' rights, she remembers that Sylvia got the Tauranga newspaper to publish a poem of hers back then. This event—in the early 1950s—opened a child from the *Pa* (Maori tribal land) to the remarkable possibility that the larger world would hear her.

Hinewirangi's sister, Parahaka, also talked with me about being Sylvia's pupil. Her experience was different from her sister's. Sylvia had not perceived Parahaka as talented, and hadn't put her forward for recognition. I asked, "Do you think Sylvia had respect for Maori people?" and Parahaka said "No." I was saddened to hear this, because I had hoped that Sylvia's attempts to reach across racial walls had been more successful. Just then something interrupted us. When we resumed the interview I'd had time to develop a follow-up question. I asked her, "Do you think Sylvia had respect for Pakeha people?" Parahaka said "No, she only respected people she thought were talented." Then, with great relief, I asked, "So she was a snob, rather than a racist?" And Parahaka said, "Yes."

Snobbery went along with Sylvia's passion for art and excellence. What she demanded of herself she demanded of others.[25] Her attitude apparently fired up her talented students, and made some of the others unhappy.

From the consciousness of the 1990s we can find shortcomings in Sylvia's elitist attitudes as a teacher from 1933 to 1957. She disdained or ignored people she thought lacked talent, of whatever color or class. She was excited by an invitation to dine with the Queen of England and put together several editions of a memento of the occasion. She was inordinately interested in her father's lineage, back to the losing side in the War of the Roses. She preferred European culture to New Zealand culture, Pakeha or Maori, and male company to female. We see in *Spearpoint* that she preferred the intimate organic imagery of Maori children to the more public, ordinary and conventional television-generated imagery of her Aspen Colorado children. Yet for all her snobbery, Sylvia championed the true expression of self.

Sylvia learned from her father's example to tell stories that validated her self, the children and us. She helped us to teach across cultures, perhaps our most crucial task. Because we learn from Sylvia to listen to the children and their parents, we can go forward, testing our environments and combining what we learn with our own best understanding. We can learn to tell our stories too.

NOTES TO CHAPTER SIX

1. "The Site of Memory" in Zinsser, William, ed., *Inventing the Truth: The Art and Craft of Memoir*, Boston, Houghton Mifflin, 1987.

2. *Potiki*, Auckland, Penguin, 1986.

3.She called *Myself* and *I Passed This Way* autobiographies. She wrote *Teacher* about her own teaching, and fictionalized it in *Spinster. Spearpoint* is about her teaching in Colorado. *O Children of the World...* is a collection of her stories and songs for children. *Greenstone* is a novel about a family like her own family of origin. *Three* is a thinly disguised report on the tensions between herself, her son Elliot and her daughter-in-law during her son's illness. *Bell Call* is a novel about a neighbor and her child, and the battle she had with the authorities to keep the child out of school. *Stories From the River* is a collection of short stories, many of them sketches for *Greenstone*. Only *Incense to Idols, another novel*, isn't about her life, but I believe it is a fantasy of what her life would have been had she chosen to stay single and be an artist.

4. The Maori *taniwha* is particularly fierce and is said to live in the Wanganui River (setting for *Greenstone*) among other places.

5. Published first in 1959.

6. SA-W to Robert Gottlieb, January 22, 1960.

7. *James K. Baxter as Critic*, ed. Frank McKay, Heinemann, 1978, page 198.

8. *James K. Baxter as Critic*, ed. Frank McKay, Heinemann, 1978, page 199.

9. *Incense to Idols*, page 154.

10. *I Passed This Way*, pages 158-9.

11. *Greenstone*, pages 103-4.

12. *Greenstone*, page 97.

13. *Greenstone*, page 106.

14. Endeavour TV, *Sylvia Ashton-Warner*. National Film Library, Wellington, New Zealand.

15. *Sylvia! The Biography of Sylvia Ashton-Warner*, Auckland, Viking Penguin, 1988.

16. *Sylvia! The Biography of Sylvia Ashton-Warner*, Auckland, Viking Penguin, 1988, page 33.

17. See Chapter Four.

18. See Chapter Three.

19. *Sylvia! The Biography of Sylvia Ashton-Warner*, Auckland, Viking Penguin, 1988, page 27.

20. Personal communication, 1987.

21. *Teacher*, page 150.

22. Personal communication, 1988.

23. I have come to take this principle beyond ethnicity, and now believe that the inevitable gap in years between any adult and any child *is* a cultural gulf and that following the child's passions and rhythms enhances the relationship between any adult and any child.

24. This extraordinary rule, explicitly prohibiting reading for pleasure during school hours, was in effect for most of my public school teaching years.

25. Her friend, Joy Alley, told me in 1990 that Sylvia had wanted her to read all the books by one author before moving on, as Sylvia herself tried to do. Her piano student, Greg Tata, told me in 1990 that he had been held to an extremely high standard by Sylvia.

SEVEN—TELLING OUR OWN STORIES: WHEN THE HEART TRANSLATES THE FACTS, MYTHS ARE BORN

[Therapy] works against the historical influences of childhood and society in order to uncover a true ahistorical self and free it.
—James Hillman[1]

The way we tell our story is the way we form our therapy.
—Patricia Berry[2]

Women and men who tell compelling stories are healing teachers who help us get our terrors and hopes out of their secret places and into the light of day. Teaching through metaphor transcends culture and fascinates learners regardless of their degree of sophistication or education. "I have a story like your story," the teacher says. "Maybe it will shed some light for you." And that is the way we teach.

We rarely have campfires any more, so finding a place for reweaving stories into our communities is a challenge. The stories of Nadine Gordimer, Ann Cameron, Joseph Campbell, Sandra Cisneros, Patricia Grace, Joanne Greenberg, Gabriel Garcia Marquez, Isabel Allende, Alice Walker and others help us to move once again toward rich and complex cultural images and connections.

In his powerful book, *The Call of Stories,*[3] psychiatrist and social critic Robert Coles tells stories about his teacher, William Carlos Williams, a great poet and also a physician, who taught that:

> ...the ultimate test of a person's worth as a doctor or teacher or lawyer has to do not only with what he or she knows, but with how he or she behaves with another person, the patient or student or client.[4]

Coles continues in his own voice:

> He was reminding me that we weren't talking only of an intellectual question. We were searching for a reliable thoroughfare, maybe—a direct passage from the world of thinking to that of day-to-day living. If we would find no road for everyone, we might at least prompt a substantial number to make the trip through the kind of "enchantment," as he put it, a novelist such as Dickens offers a willing reader....Perhaps Williams was overly confident that somehow the storyteller can exert a pull on readers strong enough to win them over to a way of getting on with others that is morally inspired ...Still, as

the old doctor kept saying, "We have to keep making the effort" and "the more palpable the connection between the story and the reader's story, the better the chance that something will happen."[5]

Later, Coles discusses what such stories do:

> . . .a story is not an idea, though there most certainly are ideas in stories; . . .reading a story is not like memorizing facts. We talked of the mind's capacity to analyze. This capacity—to abstract, to absorb elements of knowledge, and to relinquish them in statements, verbal or written—is an important part of what we are: creatures of language, of symbols galore. But we need not use ourselves, so to speak, in only that way. . . .We have memories; we have feelings. We reach out to others. We have the responsiveness that one sees in preliterate infants who cry when others cry, smile when others smile, frown when others frown; or the responsiveness of youngsters, even preschool ones, who sing in response to the sound of others singing, who get choked up when shown a sad picture or told about a sad event. That side of ourselves is not set apart from our intellect. In order to respond, one remembers, one notices, then one makes connections—engaging the thinking mind as well as what is called one's emotional side.
>
> How to encompass in our minds the complexity of some lived moments in a life? How to embody in language the mix of heightened awareness and felt experience which reading a story can end up offering to the reader?[6]

Coles is teaching explicitly what Sylvia taught implicitly: there are stories that are truer than the literal truth. Often *il*-logical (not sensible to the mind) by everyday standards, stories are nevertheless *psycho-*logical (sensible to the spirit) and, as we will see, *mytho-*logical (sensible to the image- or legend-maker). They are from the side of the mind that dreams and jumps to conclusions, that embraces metaphor and feels empathy. Sylvia, raised on stories, made them, apparently, with little effort. I never thought of myself as the kind of storyteller who makes up stories, but now I have learned that I am.

Transforming fact to story is one kind of mythologizing. We shift the facts as we remember them into the part of the mind—the home of poetic license—that uses symbols to say things more truly and wonderfully than history can. Story making shifts the story from the mind to the soul, from the credible to the incredible, from fact to truth. Jean Houston has said: "A myth is something that never happened but is happening all the time." Mythologizing puts the emotional significance back into history, restoring meaning that we don't see in the unmythologized "facts."[7]

Webster's Ninth New Collegiate Dictionary[8] defines a myth as "a traditional story of an ostensibly historical event that serves to unfold part of the world view of a people or to explain a belief." Another definition comes from anthropology:

> Myths are accounts about how the world came to be the way it is, about a super-ordinary realm of events before (or behind) the experienced natural world; they are accounts believed to be true and in some sense sacred.[9]

Sylvia seems to have kept herself just this side of madness by making personal myths: taking the hard events of her life and transforming them into creative stories and empathetic teaching. Safeguarding herself in this way enhanced her sensitivity to children and her ability to help other adults heal themselves and children. A teacher friend wrote a poem about how this works:

> I have turned
> my childhood's garbage
> into adult treasure
>
> It's better than survival.
> I'm breaking silence,
> reaching roots,
> learning skilled love
> for my self
> and for each child
>
> I'll show you
> my spine
> in the sun
> —Melen Lunn[10]

Like mythology, history is also a retelling—in this case by historians who try to ascertain and convey "what really happened." They never totally succeed, however, and so history is periodically revised.

I have discovered to my surprise that just about everyone can mythologize. As I consider the importance of authentic voice, I want to know how to make such stories, myself. The rest of this chapter shows you how to convert history into stories that instruct, entertain and heal. Experimenting with this idea has opened remarkable channels of self-understanding and creativity for me and for a substantial proportion of my students and friends.

ONE WAY TO EVOKE A MYTH

To mythologize, I need the help of a partner, to whom I must tell my story twice. The first telling is history, facts, what I experienced, my problem and how I lived or am living through it, with or without resolution. The first telling of the story is the way we tell stories all the time, over a cup of tea or glass of beer, so we can hear them and so our friends can share our experience.

The second telling is assisted by the partner. An opening, or suspension of disbelief, must begin the process. This telling consists of letting the world of metaphor emerge. Note the word *letting*. Openly inviting. Permitting. Despite our general obliviousness to it, this world of metaphor lives right next door to the home of literal meaning, separated only by the thinnest, most permeable of walls. So my partner opens a door in the wall, saying something like this:

> Now tell me the story again, but this time tell it as a fable, a myth, a fairy tale or an animal story. Say the words "once upon a time" and then wait for a protagonist to appear. It probably won't be a person, and we won't have to wait very long, but just let it come. Then let the protagonist, your mythical figure, your tender animal spirit, your superhero, your infant self or angel experience the problem, telling it in suitable terms.
> Remember to use seven-league boots, shamans, enchanted swords, glass slippers, tricksters, maidens, warriors, three wishes, sultans, talking animals, minions, younger and older brothers and sisters, wicked parents and stepparents, fairy godmothers, devils, bolts of lightening, magic carpets, princesses, noble knights, wands, time machines, potions—anything which supports taking your protagonist through the problem and on to the triumphant solution and satisfying ending.

If my myth-making partner will sit with me, listening carefully and believing that my story will come, then the transformation from telling what happened to telling the significant story will occur. The story will form, sometimes lengthy, sometimes short and simple.

In my Pacific Oaks College class on Sylvia Ashton-Warner, Maria Consiglio[11] described her problem and then told her story:

> My problem is letting go of people, circumstances. I used to know how to do it, and somehow forgot. It's hard to say goodbye to the children at the end of the year. (Susan: You get close to people and they go away, they're a part of you but not present any more.) (Alison: Is the problem that they don't include you in the decision to leave you?) It's hardest when it's not my decision, when I have no say in the matter.
>
> Once upon a time there was a little tiny person who walked down a road. The road was dusty and had many, many stones on it. The person bent down and picked up a stone, and put it in her pocket, and kept right on walking, bent down and picked up another stone, and put it in her pocket, and kept right on walking, picking up another stone. Then a creature came across the road, and asked the person to stop picking up stones and putting them in her pocket. The little person asked why and the creature said, "The stones are not yours to keep, they are there to look at, to enjoy, and maybe carry around for a while, but they are always to be put back where you found them."
>
> This little person got upset by this, and kept walking down the road, picking up stones and putting them in her pocket. She was trying to figure out how to keep the stones. What the creature had said to her went around and around in her mind. Then she saw one green branch. She walked over to it, picked it up, looked at it, put it down, and then took all the stones out of her pocket, put all the stones down by the green branch, and walked on down the road, and felt okay about it. Did she look back? No. Was she uplifted? I'd say so.

Susan W. told this story:

> Every time I've been home so far I've been reminded that my mother has blinders on, she thinks that I am perfect. She thinks everything around me is fine, and I'm this strong, good person. She likes to talk to me about my sister who has all of these problems. So we end up, whenever I come to visit, talking about my sister the whole time I'm there. But I want to talk about me, and her, and what she's doing and what I'm doing. We've been talking about my sister since I was about twelve, and

I'm tired of it. I'm also hurt because I pay a lot of money to come home and visit, get on the plane to go home excited because I miss her, and wish for the perfect mother. And I find myself wanting to escape about halfway through each visit. That's probably why I moved to California in the first place.

Once upon a time in a small, small village, there were born two baby girls. They were exactly the same, *exactly*. When the first girl was born, the doctor was thrilled, because she was his thousandth baby, and he cast a spell on her, so that she always appeared perfect to her parents. While the mother was screaming in the throes of delivering her first baby the doctor waved his magic wand and said, "You will always look perfect."

At that second, even though the baby was all bloody and gooey, the mother looked and said, "She's perfect! She's beautiful!" And the mother was thrilled and happy. And when the second baby came out she was covered with blood and blue, and the mother started to cry. And then she turned to her firstborn and said, "I'm so glad you're perfect, but just *look* at your sister!"

The children grew up and the two little girls played together and loved each other a lot. They would go out into the woods and play, and collect stones, and meet little forest animals and climb trees. One day they were out in the woods climbing trees, and they both fell out! They both hurt themselves. The older sister broke her arm and the second sister broke her leg.

They hobbled back to the mother, who couldn't tell that the older girl had broken her arm because she was perfect. She rushed the younger girl to the doctor as fast as she could, leaving the older one at home to make dinner. The older girl was puzzled and confused but she made dinner and got better and her arm healed. But it healed funny, and she could never climb trees the way she had before.

She grew up and grew up and decided, finally, to move away. It was *said* that she moved away because she was beginning to look beat up and rather malnourished, and her mother didn't seem to notice. She made new friends and got her arm fixed and people reminded her when she needed another meal. She missed her mother and sister, though, so she would go home to visit.

So one day she went home and saw the doctor-magician in the village square. He told her "I remember you. You were the thousandth baby I delivered." She asked, "How can you remember me?" And he replied, "I cast a spell on you at birth." She exclaimed, "Spells? Tell me about this spell." She got very angry and dragged him into the first public bathroom she saw. He wouldn't tell her, but started to cry, and she yelled, "Tell me! Tell me!" and flushed his head into the toilet.

And he said, "Okay, okay, okay. I put a spell on you that you would always look perfect to your mother." She dragged him to her house and made him tell her mother. Then the magician started to cry and told her he would take away the spell if she would only drink some cornstarch and water. So she drank it and felt exactly the same, but her mother noticed, at once, that she hadn't been eating and her hair was turning gray and that she didn't look as happy in her marriage as she should.

And they lived happily ever after.

Laurie Cornelius told a story. Her protagonist, a loon, was the hands-down favorite for winning the diving contest but discovered that he didn't want to compete at diving and instead, at the last minute, flew away. As she told her story, Laurie discovered that her interest is in designing and initiating projects or images, not in maintaining them. Her story told her about the difference between quitting and letting go.

One woman was struggling with a housing problem, and found she had a turtle as protagonist. Another, searching for creative freedom, found in her story—about a dolphin who worked in a tank at an amusement park—that if her dolphin-heroine *refused* to perform she would be taken by helicopter and thrown back in the sea, there to attend, much to her relief, to her own needs. Through this process another discovered that her cat became a god, and she the worshiper. Another, to cheers from her audience, slew the wicked stepmother who put her own needs before those of the child. Several storytellers traveled through dark forests into brilliant sunshine on the other side.

Perhaps the center of education *is* the telling of potent stories. Betty Jones tells that among some Eskimo people adults refrain from saying "Don't do that again," but instead tell a story of what happened to somebody else who once did that. These adults expect children to be clever enough to notice that the story applies to them.

Sylvia knew this. Greg Tata, one of Sylvia's former students, told me of a cliff-hanging story she related, day by day at their Hallelujah Chorus rehearsal, about a boy named George. On the day on which they were to perform, Sylvia brought the story to its triumphant conclusion, and George turned out to be George Frederick Handel.

While *we* may have to practice in order to shuttle between the literal and the metaphoric, it was natural and appropriate to Sylvia to tell a storied version of a happening, changing the facts to feelings' "true voice." It had been her father's way of escaping the prison of his chair, and it was hers, at home, at school, in her novels and in her autobiography. Translating experience into stories removed some of the drudgery from her life, replacing it with poetry. [12]

Sylvia struggled with her own contradictions. In her other books her solution was to mythologize her own character, but in *Myself* she *de*mythologized herself—stripping away the elegant clothing of her novels and her emotional overlay, letting us watch her struggle to become authentic. The demythologized character is less universally interesting. She is much loved by some younger teachers who can identify directly with her specific struggles, but people leading substantially different lives are less sympathetic to this panicky, torn, self-indulgent heroine than we were to Mrs. Henderson of *Teacher* or Miss Vorontosov of *Spinster*. She doesn't even shock and astonish, as did Germaine, the alluring, amoral, irreverent sinner in *Incense to Idols*. It isn't Sylvia and her life that interest us past a certain age, but rather Sylvia and her imagination. [13] Here is my myth about her:

Myth of Sylvia

nce upon a time a little girl was born into a troubled family. Her father, Puppa, was severely crippled, so he couldn't go out and make a living. All he could do was care for the toddler when she came to him for feeding, cleaning and loving.

Her mother, Mumma, was a rough, gruff, tough-minded teacher with too many children, too much to do and not nearly enough money.

As she grew up, the girl, like her brothers and sisters, spent her time worrying about Puppa and avoiding Mumma, who always gave any nearby child plenty of work. As if it weren't enough to be born into a raggedy, rowdy family she couldn't be proud of, the girl—who wanted, like most little girls, to be a princess—found out bit by bit that she wasn't the prettiest, smartest, most charming, strongest, kindest or most anything of all those brothers and sisters. Since there were so many, she didn't get the kind of notice girls who are princesses thrive on. She felt bad about herself, and swore that she'd rise, make something of herself and Show Them. This wouldn't exactly make up for not being a princess, but it was the best she could imagine.

ow it happened that one day, even before the girl was born, a fairy came and gave two magic potions to the children in this family to use forever, especially when food and kindness were scarce. One potion caused Puppa to tell stories about the wide world and the fun of it all. The other potion turned into a piano, a real piano of ivory and rosewood, much the worse for wear but able to make the rafters ring, the heart rest and, miraculously, to make Mumma leave you alone while you were practicing.

The girl grew older and bigger, drinking daily from one potion, nightly from the other, and dreaming up magical ways of transforming her dreary life into one which would better suit her.

Later she became a Young Lady and found a Charming Knight who saw her possibilities. The Lady and her Knight had a short honeymoon and then went on a quest which was more the Knight's than the Lady's, but she was game and besides, in a minute they had three babies and so she was very busy. Surrounded by babies and with no way to get back to her own quest, she lost herself down the well.

Several neighborhood wizards tried to help the Lady, but the dark water obscured their view and they couldn't see clearly enough to rescue her.

smart and savvy sorcerer from the city finally saw it all, and helped her out, teaching her to weave a rope of velvet ropes to hold the fragments of her soul and then to name those fragments and make herself whole.

The sorcerer stayed after she climbed out of the well, helping her remove the crinoline from sex and the polite veneer from fear, and led the Lady to dreams of peace and a vision of ardent learning and expression through sculpture, painting, poetry, music and dance.

She learned from the sorcerer that she must always, always, always remember her own quest, no matter how hard it was amid the important things of life—like children, doing what was expected of Ladies and living up to the standards of her Knight.

❤ ☙ ❦ ❤ ☙ ❦ ❤ ☙ ❦

It was unfashionable for Ladies to have quests of their own in that time and place but our Lady couldn't afford to care about that, and quested like anything. She survived, determined to be one who'd unearth treasure for the world.

Her husband's quest still got in the way of her own. Sometimes her dreams got heavy and she drank to keep up her courage.

ometimes her husband's quest led her to use her gifts and her own magic, with results that sounded like songs. Often she simply didn't understand people without missions, and just about always, they didn't understand her: how she acted, what she prized, or who she was.

She got even, making a new music that people who cared could sing well and prize.

Once she ran away to see a fabulous foreign woman play an ivory and rosewood piano in the big city. More than once she just didn't help her husband. Many times she did other inappropriate things, but they didn't matter because she got on with her music, was tolerant of her husband's work, and helped the three children to be healthy and strong. Her quest turned out well: She made songs people wanted to sing, crafted from her father's storytelling and her mother's respect for the piano.

When the World said it wanted her songs, she told her Knight that she must devote herself mainly and centrally to composing them, and officially quit his quest.

She ate with the Queen of the Past and visited with the King of Beaux Artes. She sang her songs and people far away began to hum her tunes, sometimes. And sometimes they rang out off-key but more often they soared like birdsong.

he Knight and the Lady grew slowly Comfortable, and built a Castle in a magical part of the Kingdom, and the Lady was proud of her home, proof she'd risen.

The Knight was gracious about the Lady's success, and for a short while they enjoyed middle life in the Castle, he pursuing his grail, she, hers.

Then he died, and she grieved and grieved.

In her grief she set out to see the World, which had sung her songs more often and louder than did the people at home. She traveled to the Past and compared it with what she knew.

Then she traveled on, a bit farther, to the Future, where the civilized world raced ahead, and she saw in it a sad lack of the harmony that had always been the object of her quest. She was kidnaped by friends who put her into a position of eminence, thinking it was only proper, but after a year and a day she found herself tired and yearning, and, after a glorious sendoff with fireworks, sailed Home to the Castle.

She found her grandchildren interesting and sang them her songs. An eccentric old Lady, she lived on, using what she could of her gifts and remembering the stories and the music, until her death. After her death, people everywhere sang better to children because of the work of this Lady, and they all lived more happily ever after.

NOTES TO CHAPTER SEVEN

1. James Hillman, *Healing Fiction,* Barrytown, NY: Stanton Hill, 1983.

2. Patricia Berry, *Echo's Subtle Body,* Spring Publications, 1982.

3. Houghton Mifflin, 1989.

4. *The Call of Stories,* page 119.

5. *The Call of Stories,* page 120.

6. *The Call of Stories,* pages 127-128.

7. A benign environment is assumed in what follows. Certainly there are evil uses of story and of myth: Hitler told terrible stories with horrendous results; wars have begun from mythical and deceitful roots. "The Jews killed Christ" is such a particularly long-lived myth. The reader is urged to make the distinction between stories that heal and stories that harm.

8. Merriam-Webster, Inc., Springfield, Massachusetts, 1984.

9. *Cultural Anthropology: A Contemporary Perspective,* Holt, Rinehart and Winston, 1976, page 401.

10. Printed here with permission of the author.

11. Students are named with their permission.

12. I invite the reader who experiments with stories to write to me about that work. You can write in care of the publisher or e-mail me at sydneyc@igc.apc.org.

13. The above process is my retelling of work Jeanne Marie Bear introduced to me. The Myth of Sylvia which follows came to me through this process. "Remythologizing" may be a more proper name for the process of finding stories taught in this chapter, since there is a sense of rejoining the flow of human story. Jeanne Marie Bear connects most profoundly with this aspect, Jean Houston writes about it, and the reader caught up by these ideas is encouraged to examine Houston's work.

EIGHT—REWARDING AND PUNISHING:
THE DISCIPLINE SYLVIA ABANDONED

... I am finished with living
for what my mother believes
for what my brother and father defend
for what my lover elevates
for what my sister, blushing, denies or rushes
to embrace.

I find my own
small person
a standing self
against the world
an equality of wills
I finally understand.

Besides:

My struggle was always against
an inner darkness: I carry within myself
the only known keys
to my death—to unlock life, or close it shut
forever. A woman who loves wood grains, the color yellow
and the sun, I am happy to fight
all outside murderers
as I see I must.
                    —Alice Walker[1]

When Sylvia was a girl in the 1920s teachers generally meted out discipline like judges, moralizing, punishing and terrorizing children. Children who conformed were usually safe; others were often punished. Since then many management styles have been tried in classrooms, from B. F. Skinner's operant conditioning to A. S. Neill's laissez-faire. Schools have tended to swing between severity and permissiveness, neither of them best for children or teachers. If children are to prosper and fulfill their promise, and if teaching is to be a work of dignity, wit and grace, then teachers must be neither tyrants nor doormats but real people with genuine interests, skills and feelings.

ASSERTIVE DISCIPLINE—
EXTRINSIC MOTIVATION REVISITED:

Today, seventy-odd years after Sylvia's school days and thousands of miles away, a judgmental system is back in vogue. As codified by Lee Canter,[2] it is currently called Assertive Discipline. When children misbehave it works like this: chew gum and get your name on the board as a warning; do it again and get a time-out; do it once more and lose recess; another time and your parents are called and asked to punish you at home; once more and there will be a 30-minute detention after school. This seems as far as the "official" Assertive Discipline takes it, but schools in Oakland, California, in 1992 were suspending children indefinitely as a final consequence.

On the reward side it works the same: do your homework, get a sticker, erase the board, get another; three stickers earn a commendation card, three commendation cards earn a pizza. As of 1993, Assertive Discipline is the official disciplinary system adopted by many school districts. Such a system offers children rewards for obeying school rules and deprivations for disobeying them, assuming that the important business of a school is what the teacher teaches by way of lessons to the children. From a textbook for teachers:

> The most fundamental condition of effective teaching, to be preserved at all costs according to the Canters, is the right of teachers to get their personal and professional needs met in the classroom.[3]

People who like Assertive Discipline perceive social interactions or other expressions of feeling to be disruptive in classrooms. They assume the classroom is for learning subjects the teacher teaches under the guidance of the administrator, at the behest of the school board, which is monitored by the legislature. The goal of such a system is to develop strict teachers who make sure children attend to their lessons.

This system of reinforcement sometimes succeeds, if one measures success by obedience during lessons *while the enforcing adult is present.* It fails, however, to help the teacher understand the thinking underlying a child's behavior. Nor does it teach children how to discipline themselves; instead it encourages sneakiness and discourages principled behavior. Such a system doesn't assure that the children learn the teacher's lesson, either, because it doesn't invest the children in the process or the content. What seems certain is that the children do learn about the uses of power.

Alfie Kohn argues against teacher control:[4]

> ...the teacher ought to be guided less by the need

to maintain control over the classroom than by the long-term objective of helping students to act responsibly because they understand that it is right to do so.[5]

Sylvia's childhood was cramped and inhibited by a rudimentary form of Assertive Discipline but, knowing no other sort, she practiced it herself in her early days of teaching. There is in *Myself* a giddy, wonderful story about positive reinforcement: when she gave a reward, a "tick" (a good mark on the blackboard like the ones the Assertive Discipline people give) to a child:

> ..."Pearly, you tuck in your feet so Bernard won't fall over."
> She recovers her point of departure. "Please I get a tick?"
> "Oh...yes...*one.*"
> Back goes the foot under the desk, "Now the other, Pearly."
> "Please two tick?"
> "Good heavens, no!"
> I'm confused. For some reason, as I glance about, many other feet suddenly stick out: the new system is working all too well. "What are all your feet sticking out for? How can I pass to see your work? I'll break my neck."
> "Pleaseatick?"
> I've had enough of these feet sequences and am about to raise my voice in authority—Put all those feet out of sight or else—but some echo from training college, some line from Freud I've been plowing through, or Jung or Adler or Russell...what was it? There's something here I should know. I sense a warning I don't understand, but you can't go around all day giving ticks for no more than pulling your feet in, the thing would get out of hand. I mean...the next thing you'd be giving ticks for coming to school at all, you'd be giving ticks for breathing and a cross for not breathing, besides I am the teacher and they're supposed to do what I say. Deep breath but nothing to say.
> Olga sympathizes. "Too many feets ay."[6]

Her observations of children were leading Sylvia to teach skill subjects—reading, writing and arithmetic—using children's *interests* in each other, in playing, and in creative media. Accordingly she abandoned extrinsic rewards and tried more sensible negotiations with children. The big feet found their way into a story, and Sylvia found herself teaching the child to read that story rather than conditioning her with reinforcers to read about Janet and John. Children interested in food were taught to read words about flavor and to compute using recipes. Children interested in things that go learned transportation words and calculated distances between points. A good teacher, Sylvia tells us, doesn't get stuck on the teaching material, but emphasizes the connection between the child's interests and the processes she wants the child to experience.

Many adults, particularly those who willingly adopt methods like Assertive Discipline, have internalized a rigid image of the teacher "teaching": holding forth, pontificating, covering the material, delivering the academic goods. This view separates the processes of teaching and learning, seeing the relation between them as going in one direction only. Such teaching denies the integration of our personalities, foolishly expecting spontaneous, passionate children to attend with interest and calm to what matters to the teacher or curriculum committee. Even when the teacher manages to command this attention, over time this approach flattens the children's emotional landscapes and diminishes their creativity.

Adults or children, we tend to behave badly when we're playing somebody else's game one we don't want to play or one which makes us feel inadequate or stupid. Teachers can choose to follow the children's interests or inspire new interests in them, or can insist that children play an adult-driven game. When we tell children to learn our culture—by "correcting" their speech to our patterns or by using only our music in school—instead of asking about and appreciating theirs, we set them up to resent and rebel.

The Maori language has one word, *ako*, that covers both learning and teaching, seeing them as a single process. On reflection, we are reminded that the best way to learn something is to teach it to another.

Children don't lie awake nights trying to figure out what will disrupt our lessons and make us crazy. They attend, often raptly, to what they perceive to be interesting or useful lessons. But they attend grudgingly if at all under coercion or artificial "motivation." Such extrinsic "motivation" disregards what Sylvia and others identify as fundamental: Behavior has its reasons. When the teacher believes that behavior is purposeful, teaching becomes a feedback loop, informed by both participants.

Children are often wild. They grab stuff because they want it and haven't yet learned to negotiate. They rage when the response they learned at home is punished by a teacher from a different culture. They hit because they're frustrated and haven't learned words to express that frustration. They knock over people and things that are in the way because they haven't yet learned the value of going around. Every child is to some extent aware of his own inadequacies and eager to overcome them, if the work involved doesn't cause him to lose face. Our lessons are welcome if they match the children's awareness that they want those lessons, and our teaching style is welcome if it is like the teaching style of those they love or is welcomed by the people they love.

Sylvia saw children's self-esteem and confidence rise when they successfully completed tasks, and diminish following repeated failure. She redesigned her program so that children would succeed at reading and therefore at school. We teachers must take responsibility for the failure or success of our methods, rather than blame a child for inattention or failure, saying, "I covered that material and this child is not working hard enough to learn it."

Sylvia discovered that children's success in school depended upon helping children, one by one, recognize what was important to them, and then giving them time and materials to express or represent it through the creative arts and written symbols. Hers was a teacher's success, not a disciplinarian's threat of awful retribution.

The colonizing attitude of most of the Pakeha teachers of Sylvia's time fatally distanced them from the children they taught. Author Patricia Grace's story "Butterflies"[7] tells of a little Maori girl going off to school in the morning, her grandparents urging her to "Listen to the teacher. Do what she say." When the child returns home, she encounters her grandparents hoeing the cabbages. They ask what she wrote in school and she reads them her story: "I killed all the butterflies." They ask how the teacher liked the story and she reports that the teacher gave a lecture on lovely butterflies and how we don't kill them. The grandfather pauses a long time and then explains to the child that the teacher buys her cabbages in the grocery store.

It is a breakthrough when teachers learn that, when confused or shocked, *we must always ask a question* like "Will you tell me why you killed the butterflies?" and hear the answer—"So they won't eat my grandma's cabbages." Nothing is more fundamentally helpful to teaching than to avoid assumptions: that the child is cruel, that she is thoughtless, that her story has no point, that people like her are mean to "harmless" creatures. These assumptions can devastate children.

As our cities come to have people from many cultures, teachers are less and less likely to know that some butterflies devour cabbages. But the teacher who has children from cultures she or he doesn't know will be on firm ground once she learns to *ask* the children and to *listen* respectfully when they explain.

Quite clearly, from childhood on, Sylvia's style—passionate, analytic and artistic—was seen as peculiar and suspect by her community. Perhaps in reaction to this, she came to respect differences in culture and sought to protect each individual's self-esteem. She invented her own way of teaching by honing her capacity to observe and listen to the children:

> All I could do was *see*, and what I could see was that to try to teach the Maori children the white reading was to impose force, whereas to use force for any reason was what made teaching exhausting and tired the children too maybe.[8]

The idea that seeing was important didn't crop up all of a piece, but came from trying to integrate what she herself had learned from experience and books.[9]

All through her teaching Sylvia looked at the problem of keeping order while working with lively youngsters. Sylvia acknowledges the impulse to control ("...once you've got your foot on their neck they're all right") by responding that discipline in traditional classrooms is subverted by two realities: "the children's interest in each other" versus "their desire to make things."[10] She harnesses these two characteristics, and imposes a natural discipline:

> The spirit is so wild with the lid off. I'm still learning how to let it fly and yet to discipline it. It's got to be disciplined in a way that's hard to say. It still must have its range and its wing...it must still be free to dare the gale and sing, but it's got to come home at the right time and nest in the right place.[11]

Sylvia examined different disciplinary structures:

> I like the picture of the mind of our child as a house owned by his soul, inhabited by his instincts; his wants, fears, desires and loves, his hates and happinesses. A merry, motley, moving company, some potential homicides, others pure saints, rubbing shoulders and elbows with one another, all together going for it, like a carnival of celebrants dancing madly. At times, from the pressures within, they venture outside into the street for a breath of fresh air, exercise themselves and encounter others, bring back food and something new to talk about, returning somewhat civilised.
>
> But now you see the unskilled teacher outside in the street come to the door, not knock and wait, but gate-crash with his own company of imagery, join battle with the defendants, rout them and take over occupancy, so that the native images flee and hide under beds, behind doors, beneath the staircase or in the toolshed at the back, where they die of wounds and deprivation. The house is now full of alien imagery belonging to the teacher. What's wrong with it...it's imagery, isn't it? But the thing is that the replacing imagery is not alive as the native inhabitants were. It is static. It can't dance. It can only do what it's told to do and what it sees to copy. It doesn't go out and see the world and make a contribution. It can't make you think and do things...and the ravished soul vacates. Absentee landlord.
>
> Simultaneously the teacher takes over occupancy of the other houses in the street, the minds of the other children in his class, so that now we have the same kind of imagery in every one of the houses, all copies of the

teacher, in a street named Conformity. As for all the former native occupants of the houses, now deceased, it's what I call murder of the imagery. Spiritually speaking, millions of children are murdered annually.

On the other hand, here is the enlightened skillful teacher strolling in the street, agog with interest in whom he meets, engaging in conversation. An interesting person at the least, so that people from the houses, the native inhabitants, are disposed to come out and meet him, exchange greetings and ideas with him. Sometimes with him and often without him, they feel free to think and do things...outside in the world. A street named Variation.[12]

Sylvia wrote about this theme from another perspective in a column on the editorial page of *The New York Times*, May 3, 1969:

We hear about integration or the failure of it between the black and the white but this healing word 'integration' has become the least honored in modern language. Far from meaning a fair two-way exchange, each culture absorbing something from the other, it now authorizes the intrusion of one culture on another.

True integration is a cross-pollination well known in botany as a source of strength in the evolution of nature. It supposes a route from the white culture through the door to the black and from the black to the white, merging halfway in a blend benign enough for our child to relax and learn in.

But where the white is dominant and the black 'placed by history in a backward position educationally,' there results a one-way route only from the dominant white upon the retreated black; a movement something less than safe in the first steps of teaching; an assault all too easily exposed beneath the goodwill in the States.

I see the mind of our Negro child as a private house in which he lives with other people, the other people his ideas, intuitions, feelings and his dangerous instincts; the speechless imagery of his assorted riches and his treasured rubbish with which he lives dramatically.

But he's got to keep the door locked against intruders on his privacy; the white culture outside he senses to be hostile simply because it is different and because teaching so often catches the arrogance and patronage of a dominant race in the disguise of zeal.

Picture a teacher prising open the door of the mind of our Negro child, forcing her way in and assessing what she finds therein as rubbish, danger and goodness-knows-what; upon which she loots the goodness-knows-what for education research, burns up the rubbish with compassionate zeal to replace it with equipment of her own, drives the other occupants of the house into darkest hiding to die of studied ostracism, and brings in personnel to her liking. Politely called education and integration, but which I call murder of the imagery, murder at its reddest.

For now there is left no route from the black culture to the white, there being no longer any black to start from. No departure point. All that is there is a copy of the teacher or a fragmented mind learning little more than the violence she herself has taught, not to mention her looting. You get the resentment and resistance of any householder to intrusion on his home. You could argue that the black culture has already been liquidated by history anyway, but no force of history wholly destroys the racial imagery in the child's mind. Only teachers achieve that.

Yet the trans-culture route can be safe enough from the black to the white; your first working material not of the dominant race but of the retreated race. Nor do you lever it out from the mind of the Negro child, lure it out, force your way in and grab it out, but allow it to come out on the child's own terms.

It desperately desires to come out in the speech inspired by his living imagery which I call the key vocabulary. This you work with. This he learns with. Until such time as his forming personality is firmly consolidated, his native culture strong and proud enough for him to leave his house and tread the trans-culture route. To absorb the entire white culture if he likes. Since he must.

No Federal grant is required by the key vocabulary. At the most some white chalk and a blackboard for our child...a ghetto wall will do; for the teacher a black crayon and a lot of white cards. At the least an area of cleared earth or an expanse of sand for blackboards and sticks with which to write. In winter or if it is raining an unvarnished floor will do to write on, the words washed off later by a cloth.

Anything our child can use to make the letters of the words harvested from his imagery, the key words which release from the locked house of his mind his captive and dangerous people. It is enough to preserve intact the personality of our child, to conserve his racial culture as a departure point. Firm on his feet now, he is equipped to make the trans-culture route toward his destination. Our Negro child is ready to assimilate the white.

In America Sylvia encountered another extreme of classroom discipline in her professional life. The next few pages show her reaction to permissive teaching, which she encountered in the early 1970s in Aspen, Colorado.[13] Working with the experimental school in its first year, she experienced deep frustration with a policy of permissiveness which seemed to destroy the disciplinary framework she had developed for her work.[14]

The Aspen Community School was an alternative school, part of a substantial movement in the early 1970s.[15] Like many other alternatives of its time, the parents who formed it were more sure about what they were rejecting—authoritarian rule—than what they were putting in its place.[16] A very frequent reaction to an authoritarian upbringing is to be tempted, as an adult, to let children do just as they please. Parents and teachers who choose this permissive discipline work hard at abandoning their own authority, hoping to ensure that children feel good, that children will like them, and that peace will be kept, since confrontation will be avoided. But like authoritarianism, permissiveness has unfortunate and sometimes violent results.[17],[18] What Sylvia found in Aspen was bewildering and upsetting to her.

At the Aspen Community School Sylvia understood the children to say they had been promised that they could do what they liked. In 1991, having heard Selma Wasserman and Bill Cliett talk about what they had seen in Aspen, and leaning heavily on Sylvia's reports in *Spearpoint, Teacher in America*, I asked Wanda Gray, Sylvia's esteemed colleague from that period, if the children there had really been told they could do only what they pleased at the new school. Wanda told me that school people hadn't ever told this to the children, but rather the parents at the new school, while not in agreement about what the school was for, were clear and united in their opposition to traditional authoritarian rote teaching and learning. While Sylvia and Wanda were also in opposition to authoritarianism, they came from a tradition which expected children and adults to pay attention to each other and try to fulfill each other's needs and requests. Wanda interprets Sylvia's perception as coming from the parents' comments to the children. Wherever it came from, Sylvia called it the "wannadowanna" and for her it pervaded the atmosphere.

In her hunt for an explanation of the "wannadowanna" Sylvia reconsidered the role of discipline in her own work:

> I look into the dictionary of my own life, where I find that because I wanted freedom of my own mind I had to discipline myself. I learnt it young. Naturally I tried the wannadowanna, which led me straight to hells; agonizing no-exits, so that there was nothing else for it but self-discipline. The other day when I used this word

to a young teacher from another country, she advised, "Don't use that word 'discipline' in this country. They don't like it."

"What shall I use in its place, then?"

"Guidance," she said.

I laughed. It wasn't Guidance that got me up early in the morning when I was young, when I was teaching and had a young family too, and had no time to study. It wasn't Guidance that got me out of bed rubbing my eyes to creep in the dark to the kitchen, turn on the light, make the tea and get out my books...discipline itself in my own life's dictionary means freedom of the mind. You've got to *pay* for life. Take what you want from life but pay for it. And if you take but don't pay, life will put you in prison where there's no freedom of anything at all.

...in school...you get what I call the consequential discipline, a little less pleasant but no less effective. "Come to me, Rocky, for your writing."

"No. I'm playing in the sand with Monty."

"Oh? All right. When you've finished playing with Monty, you can come then."

But he doesn't come and I don't call again. Nor do any of us reprove him...when we come to the reading place of our own writing, Rocky's turn comes. "But I haven't got anything to read," he complains.

"Well, read what you wrote yesterday or the day before."

"No," from Durla. "We've heard what you wrote yesterday."

"But I want my turn. I wanna read."

"You should have written something new," from Gelo.

I leave it.

"It's my turn now," from Peter.

The consequential discipline looks after itself.[19]

This "consequential discipline" looks very much like Rudolf Dreikurs' "logical consequences,"[20] a familiar concept to many American teachers since the '60s. Both Dreikurs and Ashton-Warner found the roots of this idea reading the work of Alfred Adler. But Sylvia found this lesson in a higher school:

...Life says, "Obey my laws or perish." He says, "Take what you want from me but pay for it." He pronounces, "Now there will be winter."

No, no, I don't want winter!

But there will still be winter. The seasons are part of my rhythm.

Who are you to impose your seasons on me!

Save your breath, mortal, and I'll save mine. It's below zero today so put on warm clothes.

No, no, I dowanna!

Then perish, wretch!

I dowanna perish!

Too bad.

I wanna be free and do what I like. I want freedom!

Then pay for it.

How much?

You pay in the coin of responsibility.

I don't like responsibility. I dowanna pay!

In that case, you don't get freedom. You get something very much cheaper, of little value: license, anarchy.

No, it is freedom. I know best. I don have to pay for anything. I just take it!

Do. But perish.

I won't perish!

Carry on and find out for yourself. I don't build myself entirely round what you wanna or dowanna and never mind the rest. There are two laws, man's and mine. The man-made wannadowanna and mine: Obey or perish. Please yourself. [21]

Sylvia had learned some of this from the Maori people in her country. Rangimarie Pere wrote:[22] "The individual learns that the quality of her own life and the survival of the whole are dependent on the contribution she makes to the group and on how well she adjusts to the demands that the group imposes." Maori meetings work toward consensus, and are sometimes extremely long in consequence, but inclusion is key.[23]

The climate at the Aspen Community School seemed to Sylvia to deny adult experience, causing the whole school community to live with the judgments of the least mature. At about this time Dr. Benjamin Spock also wrote about what he saw as the abandonment of authority by adults:

When I was writing the first edition, between 1943 and 1946, the attitude of a majority of people toward infant feeding, toilet training, and general child management was still fairly strict and inflexible. However, the need for greater understanding of children and for flexibility in their care had been made clear by educators, psychoanalysts, and pediatricians, and I was trying to encourage this. Since then a great change in attitude has occurred, and nowadays there seems to be more chance of a conscientious parent's getting into trouble with permissiveness than with strictness....[24]

The anarchy undercut Sylvia's teaching and subverted cooperative work. In her journal she wrote aching criticism of the state of affairs in Aspen, insisting that teaching must happen predictably, in a way the children can understand and rely on:

> There's only one thing...routine. So they know what to do, feel where to go, relax in a shape around them. It's a protection and a haven for them from their bewilderment—from what they think is freedom, if you like. This doesn't happen to be freedom as it is; it's intoxication. They're only children, and need direction finders. Routine, shape, stability.[25]

Sylvia argued with the permissive Americans:

> "I take it...that what you're all telling me is that no one is in the position to ask the children, *expect* the children, to help us with the other children?"
>
> Doggedly, "They don't like any one of them to be in authority over any other."
>
> "They 'don't like.' Interesting." The authority terror again. No wonder they go in for the wannadowanna. I'm baffled. I don't know what to do about the terror of authority. New ground. New country to colonize. In some societies, the police are as close to the people as bartenders and butchers. I sit a moment on the floor to think it over while our children careen, carouse and climb. I'm recalling other children I've known honored to be the policemen, and children who like being policed by each other. If we could get clear of politics, we could get on with teaching. Where the devil has the substance of education got to? Ah! I've got it. "Have you got anything against the word 'captains'?"
>
> No one answers at once. No one stops Rocky from standing on the guitar while Monty unscrews the strings.
>
> "You do have captains in this country, don't you ... in sport?"
>
> Carefully thoughtful, examining it.
>
> "Aren't I allowed to ask a boy to bring in the children, for instance? After all, he's more agile and energetic than I am. I can be preparing their work. I can do things that he can't and he can do things that I can't. Or does it work only one way in an open school—in an open country, if you like: that I do things that he can't but

he's too free to do things that I can't? Is this what you mean by equality? How holy is this equality?"[26]

Sylvia didn't want to cajole, wheedle or entice children into the lessons they must learn. They had plenty of time when they were free to choose their occupation in her class, but they were also expected to cooperate when she had work for them to do:

> Just say, "Here's our work; do it." or "Peter, come to me." The direction is clear and the intention is uncluttered, but none of this mixes with Authority and Equality and the suspicion in the word "Force."[27]

In my experience, the American alternative schools which survived (including The Discovery Room for Children in New York City, which I co-founded in 1971 and directed for two years; Aspen Community School, which I visited in November, 1991; The San Francisco Charter Early Childhood School, which I founded in 1994 and left in 1995 over this issue; and Pacific Oaks College, where I taught 1988-1992) have for years struggled to find a balance between two extremes. We love and shelter children or vulnerable students with nurturing permission and yet we also provoke them to think deeply and to take risks. While a perfect balance seems a far-off dream, at best the schools develop a philosophy like "Comfort the afflicted and afflict the comfortable."[28] In practice this means that we treat each child differently, depending on what we see as the individual's strengths and needs. So, for example, we try to make active *learners* of active children and to make *active* learners of passive children. My experience at the San Francisco Charter Early Childhood School in 1994-5 led me to believe that the vast differences among family expectations make individual treatment of children appear threatening to some parents from other classes and cultures, and the attitude on the part of some parents that the teacher was there to do whatever parents wanted (a friend who teaches private school calls this "teacher as maid") was also chilling.

Sylvia herself was both afflicted and uncomfortable in Aspen; she suffered from the altitude and she found that Aspen people valued odd things. The school was part of her discomfort. The prevailing mood was anti-authority, yet Sylvia was the authority they had invited to lead the lower school. In the midst of all this strangeness, without Keith to protect her from the world, only writing felt familiar.

She was frightened by the influence of electronic media on American children: It removed the immediacy, activity and magic of discovery from learning and replaced it with uniform imagery. Her analysis continues, more than twenty years later, to be accurate and illuminating:

Musing on the absence of something vital, Sylvia wrote:

> You don't get far without a dream to lure...
> Dreams are a blast from the living imagery exploding with
> profligacy. There are no limits to the dreams a mind can
> conceive, but only the whole mind has the mechanism to
> dream. We need to dream. It's somewhere to go...into
> a dream...if you're prepared for return to reality. Like
> sitting on a seat at an airport to rest. Man does not live by
> bread alone but by dreams also. Yet no dreams combust
> from imagery which is sedated or dead; not the kind with
> the power to lure you. Man does not die from
> breadlessness but from dreamlessness also. Only the
> smell of decomposition haunts the house where once
> dreams were born. Boredom is the occupier now who
> swallows up life in a yawn.[29]

American readers may not find Sylvia's Aspen children typical or representative of all American children; we know children with dreams and passion, raised both with an expectation that they will be courteous and responsive to others and with permission to express their feelings. We can see that some of Sylvia's Aspen children had rhythm and response. Sylvia's previous experience teaching children was entirely in New Zealand and predominantly with rural Maori children for whom English was a second language. In a most sophisticated tourism center in America she was trying to generalize from her tiny country with two predominant cultures to our enormous one with many cultures and classes. In the Aspen school there were children of the rich and children of hippies and children of the people who worked in the service of the rich. Unsurprisingly, Sylvia's political generalizations didn't work.

But the Community School was not entirely frustrating. When she saw some shape emerge in her class, Sylvia rhapsodized:

> ...painting at the ten-child easel,...playing and
> pouring in the water tank, exchanging soft secrets,
> concentrated engineering in the sand tank...tunneling,
> constructing and composing scapes;...hands a-passion in
> the clay room modeling tirelessly; only music is missing,
> and the dancing. It's refreshing to cruise through...seeing
> all of each child in action; his head, his heart, his hands
> and his tongue. And all of each teacher....[30]

Sylvia, wanting warm, creative connection with the children she taught, resisted permissiveness as well as bossy, colonizing, chilling, judgmental, intrusive teaching—anything that resembled Assertive Discipline. She taught us that we can do better, refusing to break children's spirits.

We adults resonate with the search for something better, spending our energy bandaging and splinting our psyches, our egos, our spirits and our minds to rid ourselves of the condemnation, punishment and judgment we experienced as children and adolescents. In the next chapter we will explore what Sylvia substituted for these practices.

———————•••❖•••———————

NOTES TO CHAPTER EIGHT

1. From "On Stripping Bark from Myself," in *Good Night, Willie Lee, I'll See You in the Morning*, NY Dial Press, 1979. Reprinted with permission.

2. Canter, L., and Canter, M. *Assertive Discipline: A Take-Charge Approach for Today's Educator*, Santa Monica, CA: Canter and Associates, Inc. 1976.

3. Len Froyen, *Classroom Management: Empowering Teacher-Leaders*, Merrill, 1988.

4. 'Caring Kids: The Role of Schools,' *Phi Delta Kappan*, Volume 72, Number 7, March 1991, page 501.

5. In a 1993 letter, Kohn gave me three references that suggest that Assertive Discipline fails even by relatively simple, behavioral criteria: see Moles, Render et al, and Nicholls in the Bibliography.

6. *Myself*, pages 44-45.

7. In *Electric City*, Penguin, 1989.

8. *I Passed This Way*, page 329.

9. Sylvia reported [*Myself*, pages 42 and 90] reading, among others, Freud, Adler, Jung, Russell, Rousseau and Krishnamurti. She read [*Myself*, page 136] about Rembrandt and Beethoven, who, by their example, validated her craving for liberty and impatience with the orthodox.

10. *Teacher*, pages 102-104.

11. *Teacher*, page 104.

12. *Spearpoint*, page 34.

13. Sylvia taught children and teachers at the brand new experimental Aspen Community School for just over a year. She was invited to Aspen at a time when her daughter Jasmine was raising six children and both Jasmine and Sylvia were out of money. Sylvia was sixty-three when she arrived at Aspen, a hard climate and culture to adjust to at any age.

14. Chronicled in *Spearpoint* and *I Passed This Way*.

15. The Aspen School has survived to the present time. It is a public charter school as this book goes to the publisher, in 1996. Its story is complex and interesting, showing the concentric rings of school reform in this country in the second half of the 20th Century.

16. See Jonathan Kozol's book, *Free Schools*, for in-depth discussion of this problem.

17. Her 1964 novel, *Bell Call*, focused upon this problem.

18. The research of Berkeley psychologist Diana Baumrind on parenting styles describes a third alternative closer to Sylvia's than either Authoritarian or Permissive. Baumrind calls it "Authoritative." Here the child has a voice, options and power, but the adult's ideas and greater experience are also introduced and given considerable weight.

19. *Spearpoint*, pages 174-5.

20. See *Children the Challenge*.

21. *Spearpoint*, pages 70-71.

22. In *AKO: Concepts and Learning in the Maori Tradition*, Hamilton: Department of Sociology, University of Waikato, New Zealand (Aotearoa),1982.

23. In the important Maori welcoming ceremony, the local residents (*tangata whenua*) first emphasize the differences between themselves and the visitors (*manuhiri*) and then progressively minimize them through speech making and other exchanges, until at ceremony's end, hosts and guests can mingle without constraint, strangers no more, and the host's speech makers invite the visitors' speech makers to join them in welcoming the next party of visitors. (See Metge, *The Maoris of New Zealand: Rautahi*, London: Routledge and Kegan Paul, 1946, pages 41 and 254.)

24. "Letter to the Reader of the New [1967] Edition" of *Baby and Child Care*.

25. *Spearpoint*, page 77.

26. *Spearpoint*, page 50.

27. *Spearpoint*, page 106.

28. Anonymous.

29. *Spearpoint*, pages 87-88.

30. *Spearpoint*, page 112.

NINE—TEACHING:
THE DISCIPLINE SYLVIA CHOSE

For the spirit to live its freest,
the mind must acknowledge discipline.[1]

...I remembered one morning when I discovered a cocoon in the bark of a tree, just as the butterfly was making a hole in its case and preparing to come out. I waited a while, but it was too long appearing and I was impatient. I bent over it and breathed on it to warm it. I warmed it as quickly as I could and the miracle began to happen before my eyes, faster than life. The case opened, the butterfly started slowly crawling out and I shall never forget my horror when I saw how its wings were folded back and crumpled; the wretched butterfly tried with its whole trembling body to unfold them. Bending over it, I tried to help it with my breath. In vain. It needed to be hatched out patiently and the unfolding of the wings should be a gradual process in the sun. Now it was too late. My breath had forced the butterfly to appear, all crumpled, before its time. It struggled desperately and, a few seconds later, died in the palm of my hand. That little body is, I do believe, the greatest weight I have on my conscience. For I realize today that it is a mortal sin to violate the great laws of nature. We should not be impatient, but we should confidently obey the eternal rhythm.
—Kazantzakis, *Zorba the Greek*[2]

I believe that something is wrong with how children are perceived in my country. They are allowed to grow up in poverty, they are controlled in school, they are the cause of a great deal of impatience and anger. This can't be good for them, and I know it isn't good for us. I know this because I have been angry and impatient with children, and have felt guilty and ashamed as a consequence. Sylvia has helped me learn to share my power with the children.

Too often sharing of power is a maneuver attempted by teachers still unsure of their personal beliefs. As these new teachers try to avoid oppressing children, they give them more scope than the children can comfortably use. As Kazantzakis found after breathing on the butterfly, eager well-meaning is not necessarily wholesome or sufficient. These teachers expect that sharing power will help them cooperate with children rather than push them about. But democratic classroom management takes practice and analysis, and a great deal of courage, since it implies trial and considerable error. When supervisors, parents or whoever challenge or question the messes which result from inexperience, teachers early in their careers often lose courage and retreat to familiar authoritarianism. They abandon their good ideas because they aren't experienced or dogged enough to persist to protect the children's vitality and to resist the other adults' insistence on conformity and control.

On a larger scale, but really with the same pattern operating, John Dewey's ideas[3] and those from the English Infant Schools[4] have been discarded by schools and school systems as impractical after very short trials. I think this happened in part because sharing power with children frightens many adults; they imagine the children out of control instead of learning to make choices and decisions.

Sylvia never confused listening to children and respecting their ideas with abandoning her own power, values and goals. She was a full participant in the classroom, and the children benefitted.

> ...I was no longer going through the motions of teaching only, but was actually and effectively teaching. At long long last after years of training, and seven years of teaching—after twelve years, there was coming to me that desirable condition where teacher and children understood and trusted each other, became at ease with each other in classroom rapport so that discipline came of itself.

While Sylvia wrote clearly that when teachers supplied the conditions for children to express their feelings through the arts, discipline would come "of itself," she didn't write much about how to go about it. Her readers have always had to struggle to invent their own logistics from her evocative pages. This chapter is my version of that process.

Here is what made up her teaching, as I piece it together. First, she gave children time for both breathing out and in. Second, she learned to read children's behavior, and third, she became a teacher-researcher, writing her observations in a journal.

GIVING CHILDREN TIME
FOR BREATHING OUT AND IN

In her own therapy Sylvia learned that she would be able to read and function well again only after she expressed the old, stuck images in her mind. This is precisely how she later paced the school day. Arriving at school, children needed time to unpack or discharge the stuff that was packed in: to breathe it out, paint it, sculpt it, dance it, talk it, capture its impact in a key word, play it out. Understanding that children don't come to school empty, Sylvia made it possible for them to focus on lessons by letting them first discharge what was on their minds.

Having always been out of step herself, Sylvia discovered early in her teaching that different children liked quite different activities, so she began to *differentiate,* letting children choose among many wholesome alternatives. With children choosing their own media of expression, there was little conflict.

Children behave badly at school when doing activities *we* impose upon them without considering their interests. They are well-behaved when doing what they value.[5] Sylvia set up periods of time and spaces so that all choices were productive, expressive and useful, and the classroom emphasized the children's creativity. She began each school day with such a period, calling it "Breathing Out." Correctly seeing Key Vocabulary as creative output, Sylvia would invite one child at a time to sit with her. Together, for just a few minutes during this bustle of creative activity, they would choose key vocabulary and the child would write or dictate the day's news.

Representing their experience and expressing their images through their choice of painting, drawing, drumming, block building, drama in the playhouse, sculpting, obtaining a key word or dancing, children Breathed Out, making room in their emotional suitcases to take in other, new images (lessons), including those Sylvia wanted to teach. She called periods where the children learned her lessons "Breathing In." Not only did Rosemary exhale her images, but her teacher, seeing their value, gathered them up, using them for texts.

To implement *Breathing Out and In* (also called output and input) Sylvia divided the day into four periods, each lasting between one and two hours. *Breathing Out* began both the morning and the afternoon sessions, as children chose from among creative expressive alternatives: blocks, art, music, dance or talking with each other, that is, building and sharing a children's culture.

By ordering the day with play first so that all the floating anxieties and violence from the weekend and its dramas, or from the morning and its pressures, could be expressed and defused, Sylvia went against all tradition, like giving dessert before vegetables.[6]

Breathing In is what Sylvia called the times of day when she taught her five-year-olds skills using the raw material expressed in *Breathing Out.* At this time she also introduced the children to what is valued in adult culture and history. These alternating rhythms organized the day and maximized the chance that children were ready for the teacher's lessons in two different ways. First, children's experiences were acknowledged and addressed, and second, children were emotionally refreshed and renewed enough, through the creative arts, to have room to take in something new.

Offering children alternate times of *Breathing Out and In* seemed to solve the question of how to organize the children's school day. Teaching reading, writing and arithmetic using the children's own interests and images solved the problem of what texts to choose. In rural New Zealand, supported by headmaster-husband Keith, Sylvia was free to set the limits and extend the freedoms she judged necessary for her classroom.[7]

She facilitated children's interest in each other by organizing the classroom as a laboratory rather than a teacher-controlled place of recitation. The Breathing Out period gave children access to one another. She would set them to play with their Key Words with a partner. They painted or sculpted next to another painter or sculptor, and discussed their lives as they worked. Hugging and singing and dancing all gave the children to each other.

During the war, in her journal, she had written:

> ...how I love to see Mihi draw. I give her a box of specially bright chalk. She draws up her chair to the easel and pours out in oblivion. It is one of the loveliest things in existence...a child's self-forgetfulness in creativity. Creativeness is routine rising above human relations.[8]

Breathing Out and In was the fundamental organizer of time. It permitted children to express what was foremost in their hearts before they had to pay attention to whatever the teacher found important.

LEARNING TO UNDERSTAND CHILDREN
PAYING ATTENTION (OR "READING" BEHAVIOR)

Having organized her blocks of time so that most children were comfortably engaged most of the time, Sylvia turned her attention to individual children, trying to see what made each one sit up and take notice. When she understood something about a child she could adjust times and assignments to suit the child's interests.

Sylvia's therapy had taught her that her own behavior had its causes. People saw her as a *behavior problem*—iconoclastic, nonconformist, seeking attention, a creature of her senses, out of step. She had some understanding that behavior problems are people trying to solve problems using what tools they have. The proper response is to help people acquire more appropriate tools.

Let's look at a typical discussion, one that could come from her day as easily as from ours. Stuart has been teasing children and making them cry. In the lunchroom, a teacher, call her Ms. Jones, superimposed upon Stuart's functioning her negative judgment. She explains: "Stuart's just doing that to get attention!" But that doesn't help to get to know the child's story, it doesn't explain why Stuart chooses teasing or this particular time to do it. These are the interesting questions, the ones that shed light on Stuart and help us devise elegant teaching strategies. Bypassing these questions dismisses the fact that Stuart's behavior is sensible to Stuart, based on something (not just getting attention) he wishes to achieve.

Sylvia knew that the search for the child's reasons is a valuable search, because to the extent that we find out, we learn a little about who Stuart is and how we can help him. She learned that when we oversimplify, calling people of any age *behavior problems* we reduce our access to them in their complexity. If we label Stuart rather than search for the meaning in his behavior we fail to find out who he is and we are unable to help him learn to behave more appropriately.

Instead of viewing children as behavior problems, Sylvia tried to see what was going on from their point of view. What part of Stuart's agenda, she asked herself, caused the behavior that disrupted the other children or annoyed the teacher? Using her imagination she asked herself, if *I* were behaving like that, what would it mean?

My favorite example of an adult reaching to understand a child comes from Sandra Sutherland Fox[9], who tells us how literally children understand our words and how carefully we must listen to their confusions. Fox tells of a psychologist who talked with Timmy, whose grandmother had just died. Timmy wanted to be a part of the other rituals but balked at going to Grandmother's funeral. "'I don't want to see Nanna with her head cut off!' When questioned further, he continued: 'You told me that when Nanna died, they would put her *body* in a casket.' No one had thought to tell Timmy that his grandmother's head would be there, too, nor had he been able to ask!"

Good teaching can't happen in an authoritarian setting where children are expected to be quiet and follow directions. It can't happen unless we believe that their behavior has reasons, and use our memories of childhood and imagination to get into their frame of mind. Listen to how Anne Wilson Schaef's client remembers being a girl:

> ...home and her church were the primary formative institutions in her childhood. In both places, whenever she was "alive"—happy, noisy, full of energy, excited, exuberant, sexual—she was labeled a "bad girl."

> But whenever she was "dead" or nonliving—quiet, sick, depressed, and showing none of the other signs of "life"—she was labeled a "good girl."[10]

Remembering her own early sense of being ignored, Sylvia learned to read the children as if they were books, using herself as a yardstick and noting their reactions. They withdrew, revolted or warmed to her, depending on what she'd done.

The staff of a small childcare center asked me to demonstrate what I meant by "reading the children." I was trying to show them that all behavior has significance and can help us work with children. An opportunity arose during the heat of the following summer day. Twenty children frolicked in two wading pools, and two more were painting at an easel, on the lawn about twelve feet from one of the pools. Steve, aged four, got out of the tub and went to the easel, chatted with Terry, a girl painting there, and then ran his finger through her wet painting. As the teachers shouted, "Stop!" and "Don't spoil Terry's painting!" he drew the paint-laden finger along his arm, leaving a blue stripe, and went back to the wading pool. Steve's teachers looked at me as if to say, "What an impossible child!" They didn't yet understand that behavior is sensible and motivated, and that what Stephen did had to be analyzed to see what he was after.

About two minutes later Steve repeated his action, only this time he was speedier, didn't stop to chat and chose red. As the teachers started to fuss at him again, I asked if I could handle this situation.

"Steve," I called. "Would you come here for a minute?"

Steve walked over promptly and cheerfully.

"If I get you some paints for body-painting, will you leave Terry's painting alone?"

"Sure," he answered, smiling.

That was that. I supplied paints, and Steve and many of the others painted happily on their bodies. Easel painting also continued, uninterrupted. Later, we adults hosed the children down, a cheerful end to the afternoon.

Reading behavior means trying to find out what the child is aiming for—assuming, in this case, that Steve wants something reasonable and that only his means are uninformed, immature, or in need of adult assistance. Instead of providing such guidance, many adults often act quickly to stop what seems to be unruly behavior without looking for its reasons, judging the splashing and painting children "good" and judging Steve, "bad." *Teaching well depends largely on finding and supporting the children's reasons.* The adults at Steve's center are learning to stop viewing him as a behavior problem and to see, instead, Steve's creative linking of the two activities the adults had provided. The adults are discovering that respectfully taking the time and finding the patience to understand what Steve conveys through his behavior is fundamental to keeping discipline. Asking themselves what Steve is after, when he does something they find disruptive, they will stay in control without stifling him.

Sylvia wrote "it seems ...so *rude* to *intrude*,"[11] and so it is. But by *using our best intelligence to help children decipher their complicated world*, and providing them with resources and a safe place to learn skills, we assist growth.

Harrold, the boy who at age four drew the endpapers of this book, was the terror of his childcare center when I arrived there to teach. I noticed early on (by reading Harrold's behavior) that he loved to draw and became calm and pleasant when he drew pictures. So when he couldn't or wouldn't stop poking children during a song I was teaching, I let him choose between singing or drawing. I told him that he couldn't disturb us while he drew, or he'd have to come back to the group. He went to draw at a nearby table, and all of us were satisfied. The other children felt protected and sang cheerily; I felt productive, benevolent and in control and Harrold was content, expressing himself drawing.

Teachers sometimes worry that if they let a child like Harrold go away from the group, all the others will want to go too. This may happen, but when it does, it tells me that the children do not value the group activity. This, like a canary dying in a mine, is a signal to me to rethink what I offer, before a greater calamity—the discovery that learning isn't fun—takes place. But if most of the children are content or even delighted with my stories and songs in the group, then I tell children who ask to do what Harrold is doing, "Harrold needs something special right now. When you need something special, I'll try to give it to you."

WRITING ABOUT WHAT HAPPENS:
THE TEACHER AS RESEARCHER

Because she wanted to make sense of what happened in her classroom, Sylvia wrote down what she saw and heard. Writing was her way of saying "No matter how painful this relationship with a child is, I can find a way to do my work with him." Writing has worked for me as well,[12] and below Vivian Gussin Paley explains why it is her way, too. But whether you write or not, you must find a way to make sense of your classroom experience. The alternative is frustration or burnout.

In a lecture called "Must Teachers Also Be Writers?" Vivian Gussin Paley defined the teacher's task as discovering individual motivations and social forces in the classroom. Here are some of my notes from that lecture:

> If an adult author among child authors listens to the children's stories and writes her own, she'll find that her own help her to understand theirs. The surprises in all these stories teach her.

> The teacher who writes goes home each day and asks herself "What questions were raised today?" Everything is supposed to make sense. If it doesn't, go over it and ask questions and work with it till it does. In this way you never run out of curriculum.

> If I don't write it down I can't figure out what it means. Talk is not enough. What is necessary is to question and argue with oneself.

> To grow: Write in your journal. Write what you don't understand. Learn to be honest. Bring out errors and misjudgments, and discuss them with the children. Ideas will flow.

> Personal private writing is the best tool for tapping into [what you've learned and forgotten] for use in your life and the classroom. You ask yourself, "How am I doing?"

> Write about the problem of the moment or the problem of a lifetime. What do we think about what the children think? Search for solutions. Ask tough questions.

Like Sylvia Ashton-Warner and Vivian Gussin Paley, if we observe and write we can learn to read the behavior of children. If we believe that it all must make sense, then we won't dismiss behavior as pointless or aimed at making us crazy.

To create a harmonious setting, the children must choose their own activities or games much of the time. Adults appropriately interrupt those games for games of our own choosing—call them lessons—only if we have carefully observed the children to see what they are ready to learn next.[13] This frees teachers from being managers, bosses or dictators and allows them instead to become investigative scientists, designers, artists and suppliers. Exciting!

Toward a similar goal, Elizabeth Jones writes of the "teacher as scribe," making imagery stand still: drawing, photographing, taping or writing down representations of play in her classroom so the children's work is documented for them. In turn the children get excited and talk about their representations, since they can see how they reflect and enhance their play:

> By using her own representations of children's play, [the teacher] can stimulate children's oral language as well as their understanding that play *can* be represented on paper. This teacher is indeed teaching, while acknowledging the importance of the children's play and deriving her teaching directly from it. Children are most likely to understand representation when it mirrors *their* own action for them.[14]

It is hard to imagine a child who wouldn't come to see the point of writing, drawing or taking photographs if these activities depict and extend familiar play!

Sylvia's theory outpaced her practice (as does ours), and even during the period of discovering how to harness passions in Key Vocabulary, she was subject to her own unharnessed passions and sometimes hit a child. She wrote about it in drafts of *Teacher*, but it was generally edited out. In *Myself* she gives us some insight into her rage:

> The thing is to somehow order my impassioned living so that I myself survive. Somehow avoid the frustration in it to release spontaneity which is elating to a teacher and contagious among children. ...No more rages before the children, no more militant tongueing, if for no other reason than it disgraces me, myself as well as them. And with no more of those verbal daymares, there should follow no more of those nightmares when I take a stick to the children and flog them to the floor... the escape of violence from the undermind.[15]

Sylvia's search for discipline showed her that making things, or creative expression, was the antidote to destructiveness. Creative teaching is also the cure for destructive teaching. My experience is that in classrooms where the foot is kept on the neck, nobody experiences the joy of learning—satisfaction of a job well done. Given the large classes and inadequate training most teachers receive, descent into bad teaching—mean treatment of the young—is a real a danger to us all.

It is arrogant and untrue to assume that *bad* teachers are made of different stuff. Even the meanest one didn't say, when studying education, "I'm going to be a teacher so I can stifle young hearts and minds!" Those who are mean started out with hopes of making better lives for children in school, just as the rest of us did, but lost something precious along the way. It can happen to anyone—even to us!—unless we regularly remind ourselves why we chose to become teachers and that good work means paying close attention to what the children's behavior is telling us.

As parents, we can fall into a similar trap, sounding like our own parents at their worst ... forgetting to listen to the memories that can teach us to be on the side of the child we nurture. Otherwise we oppress children, telling them, in effect, "I won't let you make me look bad. I suffered through my schooling (or my childhood) without much consideration, support or attention to my individuality, and so can you!"

For each of us, the model of the worst treatment we received as children lies in wait, no matter if it was consistent or occasional. Awesome in our memory, it sits ready to erupt when we lose perspective. We tend to do as we were done by. This throwback behavior leads to regret if we're honest, or to defending what we know is wrong, if we're not.

Sylvia solved her classroom discipline problems by changing herself: her perceptions of what the children were doing, her attitudes toward the prescribed curriculum and her rhythms so there was room for both teacher and child to lead. She connected with the children through their stories, and she found her discipline in story and music and in the rhythmical way we breathe. She teaches us to keep on doing our personal psychological work, to guard vigilantly our access to creative expression, and to investigate how the children can make choices that satisfy their individual needs, becoming more themselves with each passing day.

NOTES TO CHAPTER NINE

1. *Teacher*, page 105.

2. Kazantzakis, *Zorba the Greek.*.

3. *Democracy and Education*, Macmillan, 1916.

4. "The Plowden Report" *Children and their Primary Schools*, London, Her Majesty's Stationery Office, 1967.

5. Children who are unready to choose at all can watch others until they are ready, while we monitor their watching to see what it tells us about their interests.

6. *Myself*, page 235, and the chart in *Teacher*, page 101.

7. Obviously, when teachers work for less sympathetic supervisors, they need to be more creative in figuring out how to let the children's rhythms and interests be an organizing factor in the day.

8. Unpublished document in Boston University's Mugar Library.

9. In *Good Grief, Helping Groups of Children When a Friend Dies*, available through Gryphon House, Inc., Beltsville, MD.

10. Anne Wilson Schaef, *When Society Becomes an Addict*, Harper and Row, 1987, page 16.

11. *Myself*, page 23.

12. See *The Sun's Not Broken, A Cloud's Just In the Way: On Child-Centered Teaching*, pages 94-101.

13. See Vygotsky, *Thought and Language*, especially where he explains the zone of proximal development.

14. Jones, E. and Reynolds, G., *The Play's The Thing*, Teachers College Press, 1992.

15. Page 171.

TEN—ADVENTURING AMONG COINCIDENCES AND CULTURES: MY JOURNEY TO FIND SYLVIA

The philosophic aim of education must be to get each one out of his isolated class and into the one humanity.[1]
—Paul Goodman

In the beginning I knew Sylvia only through her books. In my classroom and on my playground I tried out ideas I learned from reading her work. Later, as I taught teachers, I saw the need for Sylvia's lessons in their classrooms and on their playgrounds. And then again, in a more profound and puzzling way, I found Sylvia in the classrooms and playgrounds of my own mind.

There were mysteries about Sylvia that her writings did not clarify. Before my book could take a final form I wanted to meet people who knew her when she was alive, feel her manuscripts in my hands, to learn to read her peculiar, rhythmic, beautiful longhand and even the idiosyncracies of her typewriter. I wanted to find her in Aspen, in Vancouver, and most of all among the rivers and sheep and volcanic mountains of her own Aotearoa, her native New Zealand, to build my own picture because I still didn't understand.

So, in the spring of 1985, following clues from *I Passed This Way*, I went to Vancouver to find Selma Wassermann, the professor who provided Sylvia her most eminent teaching post.[2] Selma and her husband Jack were the first people I met who had known Sylvia. They introduced me to others who had worked with her, some of them "Spears,"[3] teachers Sylvia trained and mentored when she was at Simon Fraser University in Vancouver.

In 1972, when Sylvia went to Vancouver, she was in her sixties, widowed, having until 1969 been emotionally dependent upon Keith. She expected that Selma would take over this role of caregiver. Selma did not, and so Selma's and Sylvia's relationship was tempestuous. But Selma did bolster Sylvia and brought out the best of her, as seen in the letter below. Selma was interested in Sylvia's painting, in her music, in her struggle, not just in her name and fame.

March 26, 1972
Dearest Selma and Jack:
    My thoughts of you fill me as they so often do. Yesterday was the gay Surprise Party Celebration. It had not been wholly clear to me why the honour had come

to me, the reappointment: it had seemed to be made of much *love* and compassion. But when Tony[4] assured me at his place that this was not so, that it was because my work had been effective, things fell together. [Here Sylvia has scratched out the sentence, "Which has made me proud indeed."]

When I was very young I tussled with the question: Which is closer to God—love or work? I settled for work. Because it could stand alone without love, whereas love has its reasons and is vulnerable to mortality, and cannot stand entirely alone. Work can go on long after we ourselves have gone, whereas love stops short when life does. So that when you honour my work and celebrate it with all shapes and styles of glasses and romantically labeled bottles the singing and the dancing and the laughing, the kisses and the hands are brushed with immortality also.

So that as I washed and put away the glasses this morning—the crystal, the champagne bottle-ends and the Chinese lacquered stemmed ones—I remembered my answers about work and love when I was young.

Yesterday when [unclear] and I were shopping we chose several new expensive paint brushes. Three are pure ox hair, six are different sizes and shapes in sable and one large one in nylon.

With love, Me[5]

I asked Jack Wassermann about Sylvia's politics when she was in Vancouver and he said he thought she paid little attention to world politics, but was clever at institutional politics, wearing a mink coat to see (and impress) the principal at a school where one of her Spears was having trouble with the administration. (I hadn't yet found Sylvia's Socialist, anti-war essay, *The Mutton Curtain*, see pages 44-46.)

I was excited to be in Vancouver among Sylvia's extended family from her "happiest years abroad," 1971-3.[6] At Simon Fraser she was cared for, esteemed and honored, paid well and given the title she coveted, Professor. Not that Sylvia, even under such good circumstances, felt understood. Even her dooryard garden in Vancouver led to misunderstanding:

My friends are mostly academic people who live a lot in the mind; they seem to wonder that I should squander time, money and back-power planting. To them I must appear an anachronism to give flowers priority. It baffles me when people who love me, coming gaily across the patio to my door, don't notice and examine the garden first as one does in New Zealand. Neither do they stoop to smell the scents and I wonder how they can understand, if they can fully understand the conditions for, and stages of, growth in the mind of our child when they don't see Nature's child at their feet.[7]

This concern for understanding growth wasn't just professional. Even at age 63 Sylvia was still raising a child inside. In Vancouver—and for the rest of her life—Sylvia often let that child speak for her. When she visited Vancouver schools, when she taught her Simon Fraser classes, when she worked with her research teachers, The Spears, and even at social events, she would slip into the persona of Mere (pronounced May-rray, in the Maori way), a child of five or six. For example, it was Mere who chatted with a little Vancouver boy called Duthie ("the brat of the class," the teacher had told Sylvia) as she visited a teacher-driven classroom with children separated into carrels where the teacher's refrain was "Keep your voice down." Sylvia tells Duthie during their exchange, "You can't tell by people's skins how big they are. Sometimes people are not what they look. They might be something else. What happened was my body it grew up but the little girl inside me just stayed five."

It is hard to know what to think about this acting, especially since *acting* was part of the behavior Dr. Allen and Sylvia had identified as neurotic so many years before.[8] One may speculate: Did her increase in status and protection as a dignitary in Vancouver let her act upon her idiosyncracies? Was Mere a vehicle to show adults—and sometimes children—how Ashton-Warner saw the child mind? Was her safety translated into permission to be more of her child-self? Sylvia was seen by her peers as a bad wife, and now she was no wife at all. Was her life as a widow more than she could stand? Did she regress for protection?

My confusion about Sylvia and her life increased as I listened to her friends. There was more pain in her story than I wanted to face. I would eventually see that the work she did with children, teachers, art, music and writing was the means by which she survived.

She had been seen by some as a bad teacher, by others as a great teacher. She herself appeared to share both of these views, gaining a reputation based on her writing and teaching about teaching, but also telling all who would listen how much she hated teaching.

For example: in 1971 she told us in *I Passed This Way* that she "wrote with rage and blindness of how I hated teaching always." Her editor, Bob Gottlieb, responded:

As for hating to teach: that I believe. Writers hate to write too. The hardest and most painful thing is always the thing that means to oneself Truth; when you have to express your most inner meaning, and express it directly. You hate to teach because you are Teacher; because being Teacher, you can't teach from the surface. I could teach without pain, because Teacher I am none.[9]

A year after my Vancouver trip work took me to Gainesville, Florida, where I found Bill Cliett, quoted at length in *I Passed This Way*.[10] Bill is the man who drove the car that "kidnaped" Sylvia out of Aspen (to San Francisco, from which others took her on to Vancouver) in 1971.[11] Bill told me stories about learning formally from Sylvia in her seminar in Aspen and informally while driving her from Aspen to San Francisco. I never told him this, but Bill reminds me of Keith Henderson. He is assured and quiet, and seems conventional but smiles on people who aren't. He was a good friend for Sylvia, and he cherishes what she meant to him.[12]

It was from Bill that I learned that Sylvia's papers were in the archives at the Mugar Library Special Collections at Boston University.[13] Hot on the research trail, I used my Frequent Flyer miles to get to Boston.

At the Mugar Special Collections, I sat surrounded by glass walls and stripped of my personal belongings, which were taken from me as a condition of entering, in a room always either too hot or much too cold, intermittently glowered at by the gentleman in charge. Before me were a dozen or so cardboard boxes. Sylvia had give the Mugar more than thirty boxes, but only a portion was made available at one time. I found Sylvia's unpublished novels. They were not as good as the published ones but permitted me further acquaintance with some of the characters I'd already met. There were also planning notebooks for the novels; letters, received, sent and unsent; plays and calendars.

Then I came upon what I now think of as: ☞THE CHART!☜ I was flabbergasted at its importance. I knew from reading Sylvia's autobiography that when she was reconstructing her personality after her breakdown, she had taken the bits of her personality out and made a chart of them, spread upon the table. Now I had found that chart. It let me look over Dr. Allen's shoulder and watch Sylvia in process. Trying to read it in Sylvia's spidery handwriting was frustrating, but I knew it was a self-portrait at Sylvia's most crucial time.

So far I had met her North American friends and looked at her papers. But I had never talked with Maori people nor did I know Pakeha

New Zealand or the countryside in which Sylvia had lived all but four years of her life. It was time to go to her country. In 1987 I began planning my first trip to New Zealand. When a Sylvia Society member invited me to her quilting society's potluck to be held in nearby Berkeley, California, for thirty-two New Zealand quilters, I brought my best potluck salad and wore a badge that said: "I'm coming to New Zealand. Please talk to me!" I left that potluck with several generous and gracious invitations and, as a result, stayed in guest rooms festooned with glorious patchwork quilts on both my 1988 and 1990 trips to Aotearoa.

Sylvia's country was full of new images for me. Imagine walking over a great, green hill in the South Pacific and seeing more than a hundred men dressed in white shirts and shorts, playing cricket! I had never stopped to picture British colonialism before, not even when Sylvia had described her country as wearing a crinoline over its head. I saw lots of grazing land. Towering, holy mountains. Hills with nothing but green on them, or sheep and green. Tree ferns and bottlebrush clumps and birds I'd never seen before. I found myself looking at Auckland from atop the hill where Sylvia and Keith had made love fifty years earlier, seeing the city made of one-family homes which go on and on forever. I went to stay in Napier, with one of the quilters, and visited Fernhill School, a Maori bilingual school now called Omahu. I think Sylvia would have been excited by bilingual programming. Napier was rebuilt, mostly in Art Deco, after a 1931 earthquake and fire. A class of seven-year-old children I visited there drew me truly memorable pictures of their Botanical Garden and the statue, The Spirit of Napier. I spent a week in the Wairarapa, a sparsely populated area of open rangeland and a breathtaking coast, where Sylvia had lived during high school.

Everywhere I went in New Zealand, everything stopped for sport and twice a day for tea. Libraries in small cities were better than many in large cities in my own country. Everyone in Aotearoa was able to swim; swimming is part of the regular curriculum. To be a credentialed teacher, you must be able to teach swimming. One is never more than 70 miles from water. Very few meals are taken in restaurants; people eat at home. There is an enormous mix of people—from Tonga and Fiji and Samoa and Cambodia and more. There is a large community concerned with learning about diverse cultures. I saw many gardens with beautiful flowers and abundant fruit. My sense was that the children were livelier and had greater security than I am used to. I got the impression that the adults were concerned about the community's children.

In my search for Sylvia I met many Maori people, attended Maori ceremonies and cultural events, saw Maori carving and weaving and dance, and heard Maori music and speeches. I visited bilingual elementary classrooms in several cities and towns and several early childhood language nests (*Kohanga Reo*).[14]

I didn't know, as I began this exploration, how much I would learn from Maori people—how much any European-American can learn. I thought about how Maori culture affected Sylvia's work. Is it beside the point that Sylvia taught Maori children? I don't think so. The oral tradition and the great arts tradition of the Maori supported and linked with Sylvia's own gifts of language and art. The intimate collective community (the *iwi*) and the extended family (the *whanau*) sheltered and accepted their members and expected disciplined behavior from them. These were values Sylvia shared. Maori people's stories were as crucial to their well-being as Sylvia's were to hers.

On both trips I met with Sylvia's daughter Jasmine who, with her husband, Bill Beveridge, was kind, hospitable and helpful, remembering Sylvia with devotion. Jasmine talked to me about Sylvia's last illness and gave me the address in England of brother Elliot, a "fan of [his] mother's work"; I corresponded with him there and later in New Zealand. Their brother Ashton is in the United Arab Emirates, and I haven't gone there yet. My second visit to Jasmine was with Hinewirangi, the Maori poet and activist who, as a child, was Sylvia and Keith's pupil. It was interesting to hear the two women reminisce, and especially to hear the warmth in their voices as they talked about Keith Henderson.

I had a lot to learn in Aotearoa, a small country, two islands with a population one-third that of New York City and a land mass about equal to that of California. New Zealanders can know their whole country much better than any of us can know the United States. For example, people in early education there knew virtually everyone in early education, and people thinking about Maori-Pakeha communication all knew each other too. I was in Hamilton, reading *Talking Past Each Other!? Problems of Cross-Cultural Communication*, when Claire Keay, who had worked for the New Zealand Education Department, told me she knew one of the authors, Joan Metge, and asked if I would like to meet her. Of course I did, so Claire arranged a visit to Joan in Wellington, a five-hour drive away.

I was amazed as one New Zealand friend linked with another: Joan arranged for me to meet with Jim Collinge, who knew a bit about Sylvia and a great deal about Herbert Read. Jim, in turn, led me to Frank Rogers, the archivist who catalogued Sylvia's New Zealand papers. Eventually Frank sent an early draft of this manuscript to Sylvia's friend, educator Jack Shallcrass, who offered me encouragement. My sense of research was gently altered by these generous people. It reminded me of the way Sylvia had of encouraging children to help other children.

Greenstone is my favorite of Sylvia's novels, so of course I went to Pipiriki, smallest of remote Maori villages, where the Hendersons had lived on the Wanganui River. The people I met there were as unbelievable as Sylvia had written:

> [*Greenstone* was...] a stormy saga of brown versus white in several parts....They [publishers] all say the characters are not credible and since they were all portrayed live from the River, of course they weren't. No one was credible there and I couldn't make them so.[15]

When I visited, the people were still remarkably larger than life and the River was still the beating heart of Pipiriki, unchanged since *Greenstone.* On that scorching, breathless day I entered a myth, underwent tests of courage, patience and endurance, and found obscure magic words I must fathom clearly before I could break through a conspiracy of reluctance so as to accomplish even the simplest of tasks:

> At nine A.M. in a small town nearby, a Pakeha travel advisor, who lived in tiny Pipiriki but worked in sophisticated tourist Raetihi helped me telephone a public official in Pipiriki. This official promised me to be at his post in an hour, but at ten I could find him nowhere in the town. Waiting, I felt invisible. Trying to regain my balance and suffering from the heat, I wandered down to Sylvia's river and had a swim. When I came back to town at noon a rally of classic cars had parked along the road, their owners just unpacking their picnic baskets. The cars and scene were purest 1940 and added to my sense that time had stopped.
>
> Around two o'clock the elusive official made a cameo appearance, told me who had keys to the school, and agreed that at four o'clock he would help me make photocopies before I left town. When I went to the person supposed to have the keys, she walked me to the locked school and then said the keys were with someone who was out of town. Perhaps I could come back another day. I finally located someone with keys, but she didn't have them with her. She asked her granddaughter to climb the hill and get them, but the sultry teenaged girl clearly preferred to sit with rapt young men in the sun and converse most intimately.
>
> Sylvia always conveyed an atmosphere of sex just around the corner in her novels, and Michael Firth

certainly wrote that into his movie—and here it was, before my very eyes on a seven-hour visit!

When the keys finally came, the grandmother gave me her whole ring, perhaps fifty or sixty keys, isolating the one that would open the schoolhouse and permit me to search for the logbook. I found myself magically transformed from one unworthy of trust to one who could hold every key in the town! Holding the keys sweatily—I feared they would dematerialize before I got them back, so great was the atmosphere of magic and mystery—I returned to the school and read Keith's handwriting for half an hour. It was time to copy the log and return the keys, but at four I again found the official missing and ended up "stealing" the Pipiriki School Logbook, dropping off the keys with relief and leaving Pipiriki. I took the Log into Raetihi, the nearest town, copied it and then entrusted it to the travel advisor who had helped me in the morning, who promised to return it at day's end.

I left Pipiriki changed, disoriented by the oldtime cars and their drivers, and the people who lived in Pipiriki. Not mythologizing at all in *Greenstone*, Sylvia had simply reported the unlikely story. These figures were indeed drawn from life.

Examining my photocopies of the Pipiriki School Logbook from 1944—sadly, the earlier ones were missing—I found entries by Keith about Sylvia:

> July 17th. This week we are having an Art Drive. The timetable is completely revised to allow Mrs. Henderson to have the full morning with the Standards 3-6. I take the Primers Standard 1-2 for Phys. Ed. Oral Expression Dramatic Work etc.

> July 24th. Last week was such a success that I propose to continue for another week. Some excellent results in Art have been produced. We are indeed fortunate to have a person of Mrs. Henderson's talent in Art on the staff.

> Dec. 18th. On Friday night last, Dec. 15th, we held our children's fancy dress ball. It was an outstanding success due mainly to the willing co-operation of parents and the excellent help given by Mrs. Henderson and members of the school committee.

> March 9th. [1945] Today was my last day at the Pipiriki school. My furniture was taken to Raetihi this morning by the Raetihi Carrying Company on the first

stage of its journey. We leave tomorrow morning by bus en route to the Waiomatatini Native School.

That was Keith's last entry. Two entries by the new Headmaster are of some interest:

> March 19th, 1945. H.T. Rimmer arrived and commenced duties at 1:30 p.m. Mr. Simpson handed over. School and records are in excellent order.
> March 26th. At the weekly full body inspection 16 pupils had dirty heads. Kerosene treatment to be carried out at home.

Sylvia was much more of a heroine, and her work more important, in my country than in her own. While she was in Aspen in 1971, she was invited to join the faculty at Pacific Oaks College in Pasadena.[16] She was also invited by Cornell to teach there after Simon Fraser.[17] But in her own land she had no similar offers, and on my trips, I heard Sylvia regularly disparaged. Some of these opinions seemed oversimplified, others farfetched, distorted or dishonest. I heard a welter of views, favorable and unfavorable, credible and incredible, and had to deal fairly with opinions which were sad and sometimes shocking. For example, a letter sent to me in November of 1989 by a high-ranking member of the Department of Education, said in part:

> It should be borne in mind when approaching people in New Zealand that Sylvia Ashton-Warner's methods were not innovative to New Zealand. She practiced teaching methods commonly used by many teachers of her time. I think this is one reason why New Zealand has not given her the same recognition as she gained in the United States.[18]

My confusion about Sylvia increased. What, I wondered, can have produced the "she wasn't special" attitude so many Pakeha (white) New Zealanders have toward Sylvia?

An answer began to emerge as I traveled in her country. Interviewing people there I heard more about Sylvia's eccentricity:

> "She just sat in the living room, talking with us while Keith got the tea."
> "She would read to us for hours and hours from her new book."

> "She never taught children." ("What?" I reacted.) "No, never. She was a good enough writer, but she made it all up." (This from a Professor of Education!)

And, recurrently,

> "We all taught like that, then. I don't know what all the fuss is over her."

Visiting New Zealand, I stayed with many families, mostly Pakeha, some of them rather unconventional, many of them with feminist members. In no case did I see a married man prepare a meal alone...although several times I saw cooperation between wife and husband in the kitchen. The arrangement between Keith and Sylvia would, even today, be atypical in New Zealand.

Marianne Wolman, Faculty Emerita from Pacific Oaks College, had read and admired *Teacher, Spinster* and *Incense to Idols*. She visited Sylvia and Keith at Bethlehem Maori School in 1964. Keith was still headmaster but Sylvia no longer taught. Marianne remarked on several of Sylvia's peculiarities:

> I got a letter from New Zealand, not signed by Sylvia, signed by Kate something or other. The letter said that Sylvia Ashton-Warner didn't reply to mail, [Sylvia] would be delighted to see me in New Zealand, and would I please call after 6 o'clock PM when her husband would answer the phone, because she doesn't answer the phone.[19]

On arrival:

> [Sylvia] didn't pay any attention to me at all, she hugged my husband and said, "Oh! You must be her husband! What is your name?" I stood there sort of perplexed. He told her his name was Otto, she gave him a big hug and then she turned around and shook my hand and said "Come in."[20]

The day she met the Hendersons, Marianne Wolman wrote to her daughter that Sylvia:

> ...may be in her late fifties or early sixties, is very exuberant, has beautiful features, in a strangely "devastated" face. I believe she had had several drinks before we arrived, but you cannot possibly imagine the

fuss she made over us, the welcome hug she gave us. We had dinner in a small dining room, the table set with such loving care, candles and newly polished silver, a young, very handsome Maori girl served our dinner (which was excellent) and then we went into the lounge,—Sylvia had invited so many people to meet "the professor" from America that I was embarrassed.[21]

After dinner:

> New Zealand walked in. I mean there were teachers and accountants—my husband is an accountant—a judge, stenographers, girls who work in factories, I mean a cross-section of white New Zealand I would never have gotten to know. We talked for hours and hours...Then she gave me a sign and took me out to her workroom, what she called "the shop"...[22]

In the workroom Sylvia asked Marianne to explain the popularity of her books in the United States and the slighting of them in New Zealand. Marianne comforted her, reminding her that a "prophet is without honor in his own country." They talked until one-thirty in the morning, rejoined the other guests, and then Sylvia, despite everyone's fatigue, read aloud from *Teacher* until two-thirty.

Eight years after Marianne and Otto went to see Sylvia in her country, the Wolmans met Sylvia again in the United States. Departing North America forever, Sylvia invited Marianne and Otto to meet her as her ship stopped over in Los Angeles harbor, en route from Vancouver to New Zealand. Marianne recalls:

> We were at the boat on time, stood there waiting for Sylvia to get out of the boat but she didn't come. Nobody came out any more. So I asked if I could please come in, I was waiting for somebody who had not come out, and there I found Sylvia sitting at the bar, drinking. And I was dumbfounded and said, "Sylvia, we've been waiting and waiting, come out!" She said, "I sent my granddaughters out."
> Well, I had never met the granddaughters, and they had never met me, so we had made no connection. I was so excited I could hardly speak at all. They had six hours while the boat was in port. She said her granddaughters wanted to see Disneyland. It was wonderful because my poor husband took the girls from ride to ride and Sylvia and I sat down and talked. We didn't go on any

rides. She wasn't interested in Disneyland and we could talk with no obligations to anyone. I can't think of any other place where we could have separated the group in that way: with the young girls and my husband on the rides and Sylvia and myself talking.

She looked quite old. It was eight years since I had seen her. She just poured out the story of Aspen and the disaster it was, and how she was "kidnapped" into Canada...She enjoyed Vancouver very much, she enjoyed what she was doing, but she was really very homesick, and she had been gone for quite a long time.

Eventually, Otto came back with the girls and we went into a restaurant and had dinner and Sylvia kept looking at her watch and said, "I think we should go." Disneyland was just closing. We stood there and saw red and blue balloons—hundreds and hundreds of balloons going up, and then hundreds of white pigeons going up. Sylvia stood there with tears rolling down her face and said, "This is going to be my memory of America." Red, white and blue, it was beautiful, but it was kitsch of the worst kind![23]

Wherever I went I heard stories critical of Sylvia from her friends. The stories are too frequent and from too many loving people to discount.

Selma Wassermann tells about Sylvia keeping her waiting for an hour because Sylvia was transfixed as a poem came to her. Michael Firth, when he first met her, asked the woman at the door for Miss Ashton-Warner and was turned away...until he knocked again and asked for Mrs. Henderson, when the same woman—for it was she—welcomed him. Several people tell about being kept waiting for meals as Sylvia held court in one way or another. People complain that she dressed carelessly for events which were important: that she wore green to the Maori funeral (*tangi*) of her husband although she knew black was expected.

Joan Metge talked with me about her one meeting with Sylvia and Keith Henderson in the '60s in Tauranga. On that visit Sylvia ignored Joan, paying attention only to the men in the party. It is painful to look at this kind of rudeness or sexism or snobbery side-by-side with Sylvia's contributions, but it is necessary for deeper understanding. My friend Susie Corbett reminds me that:

This is only 'rude, sexist and snobbish' to post-1970 feminists. Before that all bright women did it. I can clearly remember talking to "the men" at parties in the '50s or '60s—I'd have said "Women are boring" and, though I didn't admit it, bright women were a threat to my belief that I was special. And we're hardly out of the woods yet. Where are the articles about child care workers in the feminist press?

Often her critics spoke of ways in which Keith took care of Sylvia, as if she were HIS child. It is clear that some inspectors from the Maori schools department saw her as poorly prepared, flippant, flirtatious and an erring wife.

For a long while I was confused about how to think about these sad and angry reports. Three different New Zealanders who respect Sylvia Ashton-Warner but do not know each other responded to my confusion with the same story:

> In New Zealand we like to grow our poppies all the same size, like this *(describing, with a hand, a flat surface parallel to the ground).* When one poppy grows too tall, we chop its head off *(the hand slicing back through the surface, with intent to decapitate anything in its way)!*

Sylvia's courage in daring to combine an artist's life with some of the protections, pleasures and benefits of marriage shattered the quiet of many New Zealanders. When she wrote it all down, it made an explosion they didn't like and brought her fame that they couldn't ignore. Thus Sylvia broke through the customary way of being a woman in New Zealand, and her reputation, sticking out over the heads of the rest, was cut down. Promptly.

Sylvia's life was a struggle. She wasn't kind and gentle, she wasn't easy. She was, in the words of Stevie Smith, "farther out than you knew, and not waving, but drowning."[24] And yet she gave us such gifts!

Now I see Sylvia as living abundantly despite her pain, her insecurity and her compulsion to put her own needs before the needs of others. Her ways of coping with her deep emotional problems, awkward, ungainly and hurtful as they sometimes were, allowed her to escape the fate which stalked other creative women.[25]

Knowing Sylvia Ashton-Warner's difficult personality in no way invalidates what she offers us. Bill Cliett (Sylvia's chosen "kidnapper") was deeply influenced by her in his youth. In 1988 he wrote to me:

> ...she was a wonderful, loving, sweet, nice woman. She was insecure but her charm was real, not a

mask for the insecurity...She got lots of service and forgiveness from her friends, but what we got from her was much more than we gave.[26]

Those of us who have met her only through her work are glad that she took time to write. She was difficult—I haven't met anyone who simply liked her—but she was productive, and didn't permit her gifts to be trivialized. My journey to find her has been richer than I could have imagined.

In my travels in Aotearoa most of the Pakeha people I met were critical or dismissive of Sylvia, while only a few of the Maori people I met said negative things about her. While Sylvia is remembered today by some members of the Maori community at Tauranga—her last home—for her non-attendance at their functions, other Maori people remember Sylvia and her work with warmth and admiration. Educators George and Rose Parekowhai recall teaching on the Wanganui River shortly after *Spinster* was published, and using Sylvia's ideas there with good results.[27] And the poet Hinewirangi and music professor Greg Tata, who were Sylvia's students when they were children, remember her supporting and encouraging their talents in childhood, and both speak of her as "*the most important influence on my life.*"[28]

Hinewirangi had a poem published when she was eight years old because her teacher, Sylvia Ashton-Warner, gave it to the newspaper. Greg Tata, now teaching music at Auckland Teachers College, remembers his music teacher Sylvia refusing to taint his interpretation of the great composers, insisting that he develop his own relationship with the music and his own understanding of what the composer meant. "If I play it for you you will hear *my* interpretation of Beethoven," she told him. "It is necessary that you make *your own* interpretation."

Hinewirangi told me a story about Sylvia's teaching:

> At the first rain of the school year Mrs. Henderson would say, "It's raining, do you know what that means?" And we'd say, "Yeah, the water's coming down from Rangi." [Rangi is the Maori sky god, the Father, and rain-drops are the tears he weeps because he is separated from Papatuanuku, the Maori earth god, the Mother.] Then she'd say, "Shall we go out and look?" And she'd ask us to observe a spot where the rain dropped from a higher leaf to a lower leaf and then to the ground. Mrs. Henderson wanted us to notice the path of the raindrops.

Then she would ask, "What happens if it's so dirty and the world is so polluted—where can a clean raindrop fall?" So, at lunch-times, when we went outdoors to eat from our lunch boxes, she'd remind us: "Be sure to leave a place for a clean raindrop to fall."

Hearing this story, Hinewirangi's cousin Mark Thompson pointed out that the idea of providing a clean place for the rain to fall is remarkable, since people to this day tend to think of the rain as a cleansing agent—absolving ourselves from responsibility for grooming our land. This teacherly story, told in 1952 when ecology wasn't yet a word in our vocabularies, put the ball back into our human court. Hinewirangi also told me:

Just prior to [Sylvia's] death I went to a writers' workshop at her house and sat with her and talked with her about flowers and how she made them grow. I had to go back to see her. It was part of saying that it's okay that I write, because my writing began from her work. The Hendersons taught us it was okay to be who we were—it was good to be Maori—and all our other education taught us about how it's terrible to be Maori.

Like Hinewirangi—but in a different country, many years later, reading her books—I was validated by Sylvia. I haven't yet learned all Sylvia has to teach me. I'm not done with Sylvia Ashton-Warner or her ideas. They have become part of the fabric of my life, and have made me think more deeply about myself, children, culture and teaching. I am grateful.

Sylvia's abundant, difficult life is over. Her work lives on. It will last as long as adults try to understand children and people of one culture try to understand people of another.

THE END

NOTES TO CHAPTER TEN

1. In *Compulsory Miseducation*, Vintage Books, 1964.

2. See Selma Wassermann's wonderful books on play, critical thinking and values clarification, listed in the Bibliography.

3. Sylvia's name for teachers at the "spearpoint of civilization," the United States of America.

4. Anton Vogt, faculty member at Simon Fraser.

5. Unpublished letter, possibly unsent, from Boston University archive. To this day Selma Wassermann teaches many things she developed in association with Sylvia Ashton-Warner. In Selma's classroom for teachers at Simon Fraser University, there is a great deal of children's work, all of it connected to the strong images inside children. Here's a wonderful example:

> My anty is in the hospital. And she is sick. And it is not funny. And I feel like to cry.
> —Christina

6. *I Passed This Way*, page 481.

7. *I Passed This Way*, page 464.

8. Also in Sylvia's repertoire of personae was a Mme. Heidelberg, who emerged when Sylvia was drinking what she called "lager," her beverage of choice.

9. Page 468.

10. Pages 447-450.

11. *I Passed This Way*, pages 453-5.

12. In 1992 H. Thompson Fillmer and Bill Cole Cliett wrote a little book for parents which made good use of Sylvia's work. See Bibliography.

13. *I Passed This Way*, page 481. But it turned out to be more complicated. These papers were from before 1971, and those she kept at that time or wrote later were kept in New Zealand, not available to the public until ten years after Sylvia's 1984 death. Lynley Hood [in *Sylvia! The Biography of Sylvia Ashton-Warner*, Viking, 1988] quotes an exchange of telegrams between the National Library (of New Zealand) and Sylvia, who wrote: "THANK YOU FOR CALLING THIS MORNING BUT IT IS FAIR TO TELL YOU THAT NO LETTER OR VISIT OR ANYTHING ELSE WILL PERSUADE ME TO CHANGE MY MIND STOP I WOULD NOT LEAVE SO MUCH AS AN ASTERISK TO THIS COUNTRY."

Nevertheless, there *are* two collections, nine or ten thousand miles apart. My thanks to Marianne Wolman and Jeannette Veatch, who made copies of their correspondence with Sylvia available to me. Wolman's papers are in the archives at Pacific Oaks College; Veatch's now are at Boston University.

14. The Kohanga Reo were begun in the 1980s as an attempt to preserve the Maori language (and thus the culture) from extinction. These "language nests" are nursery schools staffed by native Maori language speakers, and meant to create some continuity between the traditional culture and the youngest Maori people. The Maori community, on the whole, view the Kohanga Reo with pride and delight.

15. *I Passed This Way*, page 365.

16. Letter from Mio Polifroni to Sylvia Ashton-Warner in Pacific Oaks College Polifroni archives.

17. From (unpublished) letter to Jeannette Veatch.

18. Letter to the author from Valerie Burns, Director of Early Childhood Education, June 15, 1989.

19. Interview with SGC, October 7, 1988.

20. Interview.

21. Holograph letter 8 August, 1964 in Pacific Oaks College archives.

22. All from interview, 1988, unpublished.

23. Interview.

24. This astonishingly apt quotation is in Lynley Hood's biography, *Sylvia!*

25. Her countrywoman, the novelist Janet Frame, was in mental hospitals for many years. My countrywoman, the poet Sylvia Plath, killed herself amidst the conflict between responsibilities to family and art. Frame's best-selling novel, *Owls Do Cry,* was published in New Zealand in 1958, the year *Spinster* was published in England.

26. Personal communication, January, 1989.

27. Personal communication, 1988.

28. Personal communications, 1990.

CHRONOLOGY

1908 Sylvia is born December 17 near Stratford, New Zealand, to Margaret Maxwell and Francis Ashton Warner. This Sylvia (another child with the same name died before her) is the sixth of the ten children who lived. The family is very poor, supported by her mother's work as a teacher to Maori children. Her father is an invalid, and stays home.

[Sylvia attends 11 primary schools, 3 secondaries, one teacher training college and one art school, following her mother's career as a frequently uprooted schoolteacher. Later she will teach in nine more schools, and train teachers in two schools in North America.]

1926 Sylvia graduates from Wairarapa High School with honors.

1928 While a student at Auckland Teacher Training College she attends Elam School of Art. During this period she meets Keith Dawson Henderson, who will become her husband. She also hyphenates her name, to distinguish her family from some other Warners. (Her mother and sister Grace also hyphenate their names.)

1931 She finishes teacher training but because of the Depression cannot find a teaching position. She attempts to support herself as a commercial artist and fails. In poor physical and emotional condition, near starvation, she goes home to her mother.

1932 She teaches winter term at East Hutt School, finding it unsatisfying. On the twenty-third of August she marries Keith Henderson and goes with him to his position at Whareorino School.

1933 In February they move to Mangahume School. Like Whareorino, this is a one-teacher school, and Keith is the teacher.

1935 Jasmine is born.

1937 Elliot is born.

1938 Ashton is born. The family moves to Horoera Native School, where both Keith and Sylvia are to teach, Keith as Head Teacher, Sylvia as Assistant. Sylvia cannot stand the multiple pressures of her life and, in the middle of 1938, breaks down entirely and is unable to care for herself.

1939 Keith takes Sylvia to Wellington to be treated by Dr. Donald Allen. The children are boarded out. Sylvia recovers and they return home.

1940 Jasmine's skull is fractured in an accident and she is in critical condition for four or five days.

1941 The family transfers to Pipiriki School, on the Wanganui River. This becomes the setting for *Greenstone*, the novel Sylvia wrote and rewrote for many years. Sylvia's friendship with Joy Alley, the district nurse, meets many of her needs for intimacy. Here she becomes fluent in the Maori language, learns Maori flax work and paints a Pied Piper mural on the classroom wall.

1944 Waiomatatini school. Sylvia observes the great Maori politician, Sir Apirana Ngata. He will be the model for the chieftain in *Greenstone.* Sylvia writes and paints in her studio. She involves the whole Maori community in her classroom, showing her understanding of several aspects of Maori culture. She respects the *whanau,* the Maori extended family. She assumes, as the Maori do, that peer interaction and inter- generational interchange create a rich learning environment. At this period Sylvia is also largely influenced by the writing of Herbert Read and tries to implement his ideas in her classroom.

1945 Jasmine goes to boarding school in Gisborne, 80 miles away.

1946 Lili Kraus, a concert pianist who has been a Japanese prisoner of war, performs in Gisborne. After that concert Sylvia requests a week's leave to hear Kraus again, in Wellington. The Education Department refuses this leave. Sylvia then produces a doctor's certificate for the same period of time. A brouhaha ensues between her and the bureaucrats, but she does hear the concert.

1947-48 December-January at Lake Waikaremoana camping ground, where Sylvia is laundress by day and lounge piano player by night.

1948 Her first story, "No Longer Blinded By Our Eyes," is published in the *New Zealand Listener.*

1949 The family moves to Fernhill School, near Hastings, a "real city," where she can hear symphony music. At Fernhill School Sylvia discovers the Key Vocabulary.

1951 Sylvia begins seeking a publisher in earnest. She is looking for a way out of teaching. She tries to get the Maori Schools Division to publish her Maori Readers. This results in the books being lost—as Sylvia tells it, burnt in a clean-up. There are other versions of this story, as many as the players in it, but whatever the facts, the tragedy looms large in Sylvia's telling of her story.

1955-56 National Education publishes five articles she has written about her teaching. They are signed "Sylvia," and attract some attention.

1957 The family moves to Bethlehem Maori School, the largest and best known Maori school in the country.

1958 Sylvia's book, *Spinster,* based on her teaching but novelized to sell, is purchased and published in England by Secker and Warburg, and in the United States by Simon and Schuster. Overnight best seller.

1960 Her quite lurid novel, *Incense to Idols,* receives mixed but interesting reviews. In July, Sylvia leaves New Zealand for the first time in her life. She goes alone to Sydney, Australia, and has a strange interview there, which results in a long article in *Australian Woman's Weekly,* headlined "From N.Z.—just to buy some gloves."

1962 A film, called *Two Loves* in the United States and *Spinster* in New Zealand, is made starring Shirley MacLaine (not Simone Signoret as Sylvia would have liked.) Opening night in New Zealand Sylvia greets the audience, says a few words, and then departs without seeing it!

1963 Sylvia is invited to a luncheon with the Queen of England given on board the yacht *Britannia* in Napier harbor. After the event Sylvia makes several books of clippings and commentary to celebrate her fascination with *the Queen's eyes.* Later that year Herbert Read and his wife come to New Zealand, and stay one night with the Hendersons. Assembled by editor Robert Gottlieb, *Teacher* is published and reviewed with high praise on the front page of *The New York Times Book Review.*

1965 Bell Call, a novel about freedom and coercion, is published.

1966 Greenstone is published. Keith is in poor health.

1967 Keith undergoes a bladder operation. The operation is not successful, and he continues to deteriorate. *Myself* is published.

1968 Sylvia and Keith move into *Whenua* (the land), the first house they have ever owned, built to Sylvia's specifications on a ridge overlooking the Bay of Plenty, with a view to Mount Manganui.

1969 Keith retires from the Maori schools and some twenty days later he dies. Sylvia has been married some 37 years and is now 61.

A few months later, Sylvia leaves New Zealand, first to visit son Elliot in Mauritius with his Mauritian wife, next to Bombay to visit schools, and then to Tel Aviv and Jerusalem, where Rotary International has invited her to set up a school to promote world peace. This project is aborted when she learns that Elliot is critically ill in London.

Elliot recovers. Jasmine's husband dies only six months after her father; and Sylvia returns home to be with Jasmine. Sylvia stays in Jasmine's household until 1971.

1970 Three is published. Running low on funds, Sylvia accepts an invitation to teach in the United States at Aspen Community School.

1971 Sylvia gives many of her personal and literary papers to the Special Collections Department of Mugar Library at Boston University. The rest of her papers will be given, after her death, by her children to the Turnbull Library in Wellington, New Zealand. Sylvia leaves Aspen at the end of the summer, in the dawn hours, spirited away in a conspiracy with Bill Cliett, who drives the getaway car, and Selma and Jack Wassermann from Vancouver, British Columbia. Stays in San Francisco for a few days. Selma Wassermann arranges that Sylvia be offered a position at her institution, Simon Fraser University, and by November 1, Sylvia is living in Canada now, to her delight, "as Professor of Education."

1972 Spearpoint is published.

1973 Sylvia sails from Vancouver on the *Arcadia,* spends a day at Disneyland with Marianne Wolman, and goes home to live with Jasmine.

1974 O Children of the World . . . , Sylvia's songs for children, is published in an edition of one thousand copies in British Columbia. Jasmine and Bill move to a nearby home of their own. Sylvia develops sciatica in a hip.

1975 Sylvia is filmed with a group of young teachers, and interviewed by Jack Shallcrass, a leading educator. She begins final work on her autobiography.

1976 Sylvia begins working with Michael Firth on his film, *Sylvia* (finished in 1985).

1978 Sylvia has a cataract operation and another to remove a cancer from one eyelid. On her seventieth birthday she sends her autobiography, *I Passed This Way*, to her editor. This was not her last book. Her short stories, most written in Pipiriki between 1941 and 1944, were published in New Zealand in 1986, edited by Lynley Hood, under the title *Stories from the River.*

1979 With the publication of *I Passed This Way* Sylvia enjoys a new success. The autobiography receives awards on both sides of the Pacific, and Sylvia accepts the New Zealand Book Award in person at a ceremony in Wellington.

1980 Elliot comes to stay in Whenua during a sabbatical leave.

1981 Sylvia is diagnosed with inoperable bowel cancer.

1982 Corinne, Jasmine's daughter, comes to live with Sylvia in Whenua. Sylvia, using a false name, enrolls in a correspondence school to learn how to write a film script. She receives an M.B.E. in the Queen's Birthday Honours List. She visits churches and searches for God.

1984 April 28, Sylvia Ashton-Warner dies.

APPENDIX II:
GLOSSARY OF MAORI WORDS

These spellings were made by English missionaries of a previously unwritten language. The vowel sounds are like those of Spanish, the consonants like English, except *wh*, which is more like English *f* and *ng* which is more like the middle *ng* in *singing*.

ako	teaching, learning. These ideas aren't differentiated in the Maori language.
Aotearoa	the Maori name for New Zealand. Maori people arrived there at least 1000 years before European explorers, and were the first people to live on their land.
haka	a vigorous chant, used to energize before conflict
iwi	community
Kohanga Reo	preschool using Maori language and practice, literally, "language nest"
manuhiri	guests
Maori	New Zealander(s) of Polynesian descent
Pakeha	New Zealander of European descent
rangatira	chieftain
tangata whenua	people of the land, hosts
tangi	gathering to honor one who has died
tapu	unclean, forbidden
te reo	the (Maori) language
waiata	a song of love or work or play
whanau	extended family
whare	building

APPENDIX III:
READING SYLVIA'S BOOKS

This is the order in which I recommend reading Sylvia's books: *Teacher* or *Spinster* first and second, take your pick, then *I Passed This Way*, for scope. Then *Myself*, the struggle between the woman and the artist (written for teachers in their 20's and 30's. If you are at midlife it may annoy and fatigue you. If so, skip it!).

Then *Greenstone*, a loving novel of life on both the Maori and the Pakeha sides of a river. Then *Spearpoint, Teacher in America*, a painful book, telling of the collision between Sylvia, widowed and lonely in an alien land, and the American alternative school where she was on staff for just over a year.

After that, *Bell Call*, her novel of freedom and license; *Incense to Idols*, the novel about the artist's raging need to express herself no matter what the cost; *Three*, an unimportant, lonely book about the relationship between a husband, his wife, and his mother. If you can find them, do read *O Children of the World* ...her stories and songs for children, and *Stories From the River*, short stories published after her death and only in New Zealand, collected from other works, some published before, some new.

BIBLIOGRAPHY

NOTE: I have given the first United States publication date for Sylvia's books in this listing. The English publication date is listed in brackets {}, and New Zealand publication in square brackets [].

Ashton-Warner, Sylvia.
   Bell Call, NY, Simon and Schuster, 1964 {1971}.
   Greenstone, NY, Simon and Schuster, 1966 {1967}.
   I Passed This Way, NY, Knopf, 1979 {1979} [1979].
   Incense to Idols, NY, Simon and Schuster, 1960 {1960}.
   Myself, NY Simon and Schuster, 1967 {1969}.
   O Children of the World..., Vancouver, B.C., Canada,
      The First Person Press, 1974.
   Spearpoint, NY, Knopf, 1972.
   Spinster, NY, Simon and Schuster, 1959 {1958}
      [distributed by Heinemann].
   Stories from the River, Auckland, New Zealand:
      Hodder and Stoughton, [1986].
   Teacher, NY, Simon and Schuster, 1963.
   Three, NY, Knopf, 1970.
Barrington and Beaglehole. *Maori Schools in a Changing Society*,
      Wellington, New Zealand Center for Educational Research,
      1974.
Bateson, Mary Catherine. *Composing a Life*, NY, Penguin, 1989.
Belenky, Mary F., Blythe McVicker Clinchy, Nancy Rule Goldberger,
      Jill Mattuck Tarule. *Women's Ways of Knowing*, NY,
      Basic Books, 1986.
Berry, Patricia. *Echo's Subtle Body*, NY, Spring Publications, 1982.
Brown, Cynthia. "Literacy in 30 Hours," Appendix to Shor, Ira, *Freire*
      for the Classroom: A Sourcebook for Liberatory Teaching,
      Portsmouth, NH, Heinemann, 1987.
Clemens, Sydney Gurewitz. *The Sun's Not Broken, A Cloud's Just in*
      the Way: On Child-Centered Teaching, Gryphon House, Inc.,
      P.O. Box 207, Beltsville, MD 20704-0207, 1984.
Coles, Robert. *The Call of Stories: Teaching and Moral Imagination*, NY,
      Houghton Mifflin, 1989.
Correas de Zapata, Celia, ed. *Short Stories by Latin American Women:*
      The Magic and the Real, Arte Publico Press, University of
      Houston, Houston, TX 77204-2090, 1990.
Dewey, John. *Democracy and Education*, NY, Macmillan, 1917.

Donmoyer, Robert. "The Politics of Play: Ideological and Organizational Constraints on the Inclusion of Play Experiences in the School Curriculum," in *Journal of Research and Development in Education,* Volume 14, Number 3, 1981.

Dreikurs, Rudolf and V. Soltz. *Children: The Challenge,* NY, Duell, Sloan & Pearce, 1964.

Edwards, Carolyn, Lella Gandini and George Forman. *The Hundred Languages of Children,* Norwood, NJ, Ablex, 1993.

Egan, Kieran. *Teaching as Story Telling,* University of Chicago Press, 1986.

Elkind, David. *The Hurried Child.* Reading, MA, Addison Wesley, 1981.

Fillmer, H. Thompson and Bill Cole Cliett. *Nurturing Your Child's Literacy,* Gainesville, FL, Maupin House, 1992.

Gilbert, Sandra and Susan Gubar. "Sexual Linguistics: Gender, Language, Sexuality," in *New Literary History,* Vol. 16, Spring, 1985.

Godden, Rumer. *A Candle for St. Jude,* London, Macmillan, 1973.

Goodman, Paul. *Compulsory Miseducation,* NY, Vintage, 1964.

Grace, Patricia. *Electric City,* Auckland, NZ, Penguin, 1989.

Greenberg, Polly. *The Devil Has Slippery Shoes: A Biased Biography of the Mississippi Child Development Group,* Youth Policy Group, P.O. Box 40132, Washington, DC 20016, 1990.

Hart, J. "Learning to Read With Key-Words" in *Teaching K-8* August-September, 1987.

Herndon, James. *The Way It Spozed to Be.* NY, Bantam, 1968.

Hillman, James. *Healing Fiction,* Barrytown, NY, Stanton Hill, 1983.

Hinewirangi. *Kanohi ki te kanohi* [Face to Face], Wellington, NZ, Moana Press, 1990.

Holt, John. *How Children Fail,* NY, Pitman, 1964.

Hood, Lynley. *Sylvia! The Biography of Sylvia Ashton-Warner,* Auckland, NZ, Viking Penguin, 1988.

Hood, Lynley. *Who is Sylvia? The Diary of a Biography,* Dunedin, NZ, John McIndoe, 1990.

Houston, Jean. *The Possible Human: A Course in Extending Your Physical, Mental, and Creative Abilities,* Los Angeles, CA, Jeremy P. Tarcher (distributed by Houghton Mifflin Co.), 1982.

Houston, Jean. *The Search for the Beloved,* Los Angeles, CA, Jeremy P. Tarcher (distributed by St. Martin's Press), 1987.

John-Steiner, Vera. *Notebooks of the Mind,* University of New Mexico Press, 1985.

Johnson, Katie. *Doing Words: Using the Creative Power of Children's Personal Images to Teach Reading and Writing*, Boston, Houghton Mifflin, 1987.

Jones, Elizabeth and Gretchen Reynolds. *The Play's the Thing*, NY, Teachers College Press, 1992.

Jong, Erika. *Fear of Flying*, NY, Holt, Rinehart and Winston, 1973.

Katz, Lilian and Bernard Cesarone, eds. *Reflections on the Reggio Emilia Approach*, Urbana, IL, ERIC, 1994.

Kazantzakis, Nikos. *Zorba the Greek*, NY, Simon and Schuster, 1952.

Kohl, Herbert. *The Open Classroom: A Practical Guide to a New Way of Teaching*, New York Review Books (distributed by Vintage), 1969.

Kohl, Herbert. *36 Children*, NY, Signet, 1967.

Kohn, Alfie. *No Contest: The Case Against Competition*, Boston, Houghton Mifflin Company, 1992.

Kohn, Alfie. *Punished by Rewards: The Trouble with Gold Stars, Incentive Plans, A's, Praise, and Other Bribes*, Boston, Houghton Mifflin Company, 1992.

Kohn, Alfie. "Caring Kids," in *Phi Delta Kappan*, March, 1991.

Kohn, Alfie. "Choices for Children," in *Phi Delta Kappan*, September, 1993.

Kozol, Jonathan. *Death at an Early Age*, NY, Bantam, 1968.

Kozol, Jonathan. *Free Schools*, Boston, Houghton Mifflin, 1972.

Kozol, Jonathan. *On Being a Teacher,* NY, Continuum, 1981.

Lewis, Hilda P. *Child Art: The Beginnings of Self-Affirmation*, P.O. Box 7084, Berkeley, CA 94717, Diablo Press, 1966.

Llosa, Mario Vargas. "Is Fiction the Art of Lying?" *The New York Times Book Review,* October 7, 1984.

Marshall, Sybil. *Adventures in Creative Education*, Oxford, England, Pergamon Press, 1968.

Marshall, Sybil. *An Experiment in Education*, Cambridge University Press, 1968.

Martin, Jane Roland. *The Schoolhome: Rethinking Schools for Changing Families,* Cambridge, MA, Harvard University Press, 1992.

Metge, Joan. *The Maoris of New Zealand:* Rautahi, Routledge and Kegan Paul, 1946.

Metge, Joan and Patricia Kinloch. *Talking Past Each Other!? Problems of Cross-Cultural Communication*, New Zealand, Victoria University Press, 1984.

Moore, H. "A Tribute" in *Herbert Read: A Memorial Symposium*,
    R. Skelton, ed. London, Methuen, 1979.
Morrison, Toni. "The Site of Memory," in Zinsser, William, ed. *Inventing
    the Truth: The Art and Craft of Memoir*, Boston, Houghton
    Mifflin, 1987.
Neill, A.S. *Summerhill*, NY, Hart, 1960.
Nicholls, John. *Education as Adventure*, NY, Teachers College Press,
    1993.
O'Donnell, Mabel and Rona Munro. *The Janet and John Whole Word
    Course* (A series of basal readers), London, James Nisbet, 1949.
Paley, Vivian Gussin. *The Boy Who Would Be a Helicopter*, Harvard
    University Press, 1990.
Paley, Vivian Gussin. *Wally's Stories*, Cambridge, Harvard University
    Press, 1981.
Paley, Vivian Gussin. *You Can't Say You Can't Play*, Harvard University
    Press, 1992.
Pere, Rangimarie. *AKO: Concepts and Learning in the Maori Tradition*,
    Hamilton, NZ, Department of Sociology, University of Waikato,
    1982.
Plowden, Lady Bridget, chair, Central Advisory Council for Education.
    Children and their Primary Schools, London: Her Majesty's
    Stationery Office, 1967.
Pogrebin, Lettie Cottin. *Growing Up Free: Raising Your Child in the
    '80s*, NY, Bantam, 1981.
Raths, Louis, Selma Wassermann, Arthur Jonas and Arnold Rothstein.
    *Teaching for Thinking: Theory, Strategies and Activities for the
    Classroom*, NY, Teachers College Press, 1986.
Read, Herbert. *Education for Peace*, NY, Scribners, 1949.
Read, Herbert. *Education Through Art*, (1943), NY, Pantheon Books,
    (reprint) 1958.
Read, Herbert. *The Meaning of Art*, London, Faber and Faber,
    1931.
Reggio Emilia [City of]. *I Cento Linguaggi dei Bambini: The Hundred
    Languages of Children*, catalog of museum exhibit, c.1986.
Rich, Adrienne. "I Dream I'm the Death of Orpheus" in *Poems, Selected
    and New, 1950-1974*, NY, W.W. Norton, 1975.
Richardson, Elwyn S. *In The Early World*, NY, Pantheon, 1964.
Rotzel, Grace. *The School in Rose Valley*, NY, Ballantine, 1972.
Schaef, Anne Wilson. *When Society Becomes an Addict*,
    NY, Harper and Row, 1987.
Sendak, Maurice. *Where The Wild Things Are*, NY, Harper and Row,
    1963.

Smith, Sidonie. *A Poetics of Women's Autobiography: Marginality and the Fictions of Self-Representation,* Indiana University Press, 1987.

Spock, Benjamin. *Baby and Child Care,* NY, Pocket Cardinal (1967 version), 1967.

Steptoe, John. *Daddy Is a Monster Sometimes,* NY, Harper Trophy, 1980.

Taylor, Judy, ed. *'So I Shall Tell You a Story'...Encounters with Beatrix Potter,* NY, Penguin, 1993.

Veatch, Jeannette *et al. Key Words to Reading: The Language Experience Approach Begins* (Second Edition), Columbus, OH, Charles E. Merrill, 1979.

Veatch, Jeannette "Whole Language as I See It," in Goodman, *et al. The Whole Language Catalog,* Santa Rosa, CA, American School Publishers, 1991.

Vygotsky, Lev. *Thought and Language,* ed. G. Vakar, trans. E. Hanfmann. Massachusetts Institute of Technology Press, 1962.

Walker, Alice. *Good Night, Willie Lee, I'll See You in the Morning,* NY Dial Press, 1979.

Wassermann, Selma. *Serious Players in the Primary Classroom,* NY, Teachers College Press, 1990.

Wells, Rosemary. *Noisy Nora,* NY, Dial Pied Piper, 1973.

Witherell, Carol and Nel Noddings. *Stories Lives Tell: Narrative and Dialogue in Education,* NY, Teachers College Press, 1991.

Woolf, Virginia. *A Room of One's Own,* NY, Harcourt, Brace and World, 1929.

Woolf, Virginia. *Three Guineas,* NY, Harcourt, Brace and World, 1938.

ACKNOWLEDGMENTS:

I am grateful to many people who knew Sylvia or had information about her or her community or Maori education or Organic Reading and generously gave me their time, insight, hospitality and stories:

In New Zealand/Aotearoa

       Sarah Ackland, Worser Bay School
       Mary Alice, Koha Tamariki
       Dorothy Alley, Palmerston North
       Joy Alley, Sylvia's friend
       Clare Barrett, Early Childhood Development Unit
       Jasmine and Bill Beveridge, Sylvia's daughter and son-in-law
       Valerie Burns, Department of Education
       Margaret Carr, Hamilton Teachers College
       Thelma Chapman, teacher
       William Collinge, historian
       Deryn Cooper, Auckland College of Education
       Shirley Cranston, Sylvia's niece
       Steve Davis, principal, Pirinoa School
       Suzy Davis, teacher
       Barbara Dawkins, Ruahine Kindergarten Association
       Simon Easton, teacher
       Michael Firth, director of film, *Sylvia*
       Kathie Furlong, quiltmaker and teacher
       Trisha Gargiulo, teacher
       Bob Gray, Balmoral Primary School, Sylvia's student
       Carolyne Gummer, Auckland College of Education
       Camille Guy, journalist
       Edith Hawkins, probation officer
       Raewyn Haworth, travel advisor
       Elliot Henderson, Sylvia's son
       Hinewirangi, Sylvia's former student, eminent poet and activist
       Anne Jamieson, teacher
       Tania Kaai-Oldman, Auckland College of Education
       Clare Keay, formerly of the Department of Education
       Heidi King, teacher
       Marion Knight, New Zealand Childcare Association
       Robin Kora, principal, Omahu (Fernhill) School
       Moira Lagaluga, teacher

Robyn Lawrence, Pakuranga College Day Care
Lesley Law, teacher, Red Beach, Orewa
Helen May, of Hamilton Teachers College
Joan Metge, anthropologist and author
Stuart Middleton, Auckland College of Education
Maris O'Rourke, New Zealand Department of Education
George and Rose Parekowhai, Auckland College of Education
Parahaka, Sylvia's student, now activist
Roger Parsons, bookseller
Diana Prentice, teacher
Gaylene Preston, filmmaker
Ted Preston, who took me to schools with bicultural programs
Elwyn Richardson, educator
Frank Rogers, archivist of Sylvia's New Zealand papers
Pat Rosier, journalist
Margot Roth, journalist
Pera Royal, Auckland College of Education
Laurie Salas, Women's Int'l League for Peace and Freedom
Robin Sigley, Auckland Kindergarten Association
Marlene Sims, Pinehaven School
Ann-Marie Staples, teacher
Gill Stringer, education officer
R. Gordon Stuckey, retired principal
Ruth Tai, teacher
Ben Tangaere, teacher
Gregory T. Tata, Sylvia's student, Auckland College of Education
Mark Thompson, social commentator
Tose Tuhipa, Auckland Teachers College
Mahia Wilson, teacher
Kitty Wishart, University Book Shop, Auckland
Kath Wood, Ruahine Kindergarten Association
Helen Yensen, peace and justice activist

In Aspen, Colorado:
    Ed Bastian, teacher
    Kate Doremus, who invited Sylvia to Aspen
    Angela Foster, teacher
    John Katzenberger, teacher
    Su Lum, parent at the school
    George Stranahan, physicist/educator
    Mike Stranahan, teacher
    Annie Teague, who took Sylvia's workshop
    Bruce Thomas, administrator at the school

Elsewhere in the United States:
    Asa Hilliard, professor at Georgia State University
    Holly Bradford, consultant on layout and design
    Bill Cliett, Gainesville, Florida, who drove the getaway car
    Wanda Gray, who led the upper grades at Aspen when Sylvia
        led the lower grades
    Katie Johnson, writer extraordinaire, who knows about Sylvia
    Rick Lopes, who drew the wonderful images on the cover
    Jeannette Veatch, professor emerita of Arizona State College,
        who, more than anyone else, promoted Key Vocab-
        ulary in the United States
    Marianne Wolman, faculty emerita of Pacific Oaks College, who
        visited with Sylvia in New Zealand and Los Angeles

In Vancouver, British Columbia:
    Maureen McAllister, Heather Buchan, and Sheila Luetzen, all
    "Spears," trained by Sylvia and Selma Wasserman
    Carolyn Mamchur, faculty, Simon Fraser University
    Selma Wasserman, Sylvia's friend, mentor and "taker care-of" in
        Canada
    Jack Wasserman, Sylvia's friend, Selma's husband

And on the Internet
    Pamela Abbott, Derek Rowntree and Jill Bourne, who helped
        me find the elusive citation for the highly
        forgettable, universally scorned Janet & John books.

ABOUT THE AUTHOR

Sydney Gurewitz Clemens began working in 1956 with young children, their parents, their teachers, their caregivers and the politicians whose decisions affect their lives. In 1961 she wrote a paper on Sylvia Ashton-Warner's *Spinster,* and she has lived under Sylvia's influence ever since.

As founder-teacher-director of the Discovery Room for Children in New York City, and later as a teacher in public schools for eleven years in San Francisco, she worked with young children, most of them African-American, using Ashton-Warner's Key Vocabulary. She was on the faculty of Pacific Oaks College from 1988 to 1992. During this time she served on the Pasadena Commission of Children, Youth and Families. In 1993-5 she was founder-principal and first-grade teacher of the San Francisco Charter Early Childhood School, a new public school for children ages 5-8 based on the work of Sylvia Ashton-Warner, Vivian Paley and Reggio Emilia. Her first book, *The Sun's Not Broken, A Cloud's Just in the Way: On Child-Centered Teaching,* is used for educating teachers of young children in the United States, Canada, New Zealand and Australia.

Today she lives in San Francisco, sings with choruses in several languages, enjoys her family and consults to educational programs and parent groups on authentic teaching practices in reading, culture, arts and discovery of all sorts.

If you enjoyed *Pay Attention to the Children*, you will want to read Sydney Gurewitz Clemens' first book,

The Sun's Not Broken, A Cloud's Just in the Way: On Child-Centered Teaching

In print since 1984, and just as practical and user-friendly today as it was then, you can order it using the coupon below:

...very good, moving and useful.
— Jonathan Kozol

I hope this book finds its way into many hearts. It has the potential to change the world.
— Marcia Berman, Music Educator and Recording Artist

The emphasis of this book is on the process of teaching. The values are largely implied. Clemens draws openly on the teaching philosophies of John Holt, Susan Isaacs, Herb Kohl, and she appends a useful list of further reading.
—*Children's Advocate,*
Review, March, 1985

Her work presents practical, effective and creative solutions to typical challenges teachers of young children face. The solutions would be equally valuable for pre-service and in-service teachers, support staff, and parents.
—*Young Children,*
Review, September 1985

The author does not ignore the difficult, sensitive topics in the classroom, but handles them forthrightly with intellectual honesty, She offers examples about handling mistakes, children's feelings of power and powerlessness, and race relations.

—*Dimensions,* Review, July, 1985

Any adult who wishes his or her interaction with children to reflect love and respect will enjoy *The Sun's Not Broken, A Cloud's Just in the Way.*
— *California Association for the Education of Young Children Newsletter,* Review, Spring, 1986

...a practical and inspiring presentation of a humane and effective teaching style.
—*Co-operatively Speaking,* Review, Winter, 1985

THE SUN'S NOT
BROKEN,
A CLOUD'S
JUST IN THE
WAY
On Child-Centered
Teaching
Sydney Gurewitz Clemens

Name_____

Address_____

City, State, Zip_____

Telephone (and e-mail)_____

Please send ___ copies at $14.99 (includes shipping and handling) and autograph to the following person:

_____

Send to TSNB, 73 Arbor Street
San Francisco, CA 94131